THE BEEKEEPERS ANNUAL
IS PUBLISHED BY
NORTHERN BEE BOOKS
MYTHOLMROYD, WEST YORKSHIRE
& PRINTED BY
LIGHTNING SOURCE, UK
ISBN 978-1-904846-86-4

MMXI

EDITOR, JOHN PHIPPS
NEOCHORI, 24024 AGIOS NIKOLAOS,
MESSINIAS, GREECE
EMAIL manifest@runbox.com

SET IN HELVETICA LT BY D&P Design and Print

Front Cover
A queen is 'born' *by John Phipps*

CONTENTS

FOREWORD

John Phipps

October 2011

Two weather-related items appeared on my computer screen this morning just before I started to write this Foreword. The first reported the resignation of a well-respected editor of a scientific journal who thought it was incumbent for him to do so as he had, to the dismay of the scientific community, allowed the publication of a paper the contents of which denied the man-made contribution to global warming.

In the second, the author warned of a very hard winter, as the early beautiful spring followed by a milder and wettish summer meant that the hedgerows were well covered with berries, the usual portent of a cold winter to come. As usual, we have more examples of weather lore in our diary section for readers to substantiate.

Without delving into any of the arguments regarding global warning, most people are well aware that the climate is very different from how it used to be; although it is true that last winter, quite severe by English standards, found people asking 'So, what's happened to global warming?' . Well, I suppose the simple answer would be that the steady rise in average temperatures around the world has led to important changes in weather patterns, with the tendency for extreme episodes of weather becoming more and more the norm.

However, having just finished re-reading parts of Gilbert White's Journals, written by the clergyman mainly in his village of Selborne in Dorsetshire between the years 1768 and 1793, I find that unseasonal dramatic weather patterns existed particularly during those three decades - heavy snow, severe frosts, gales, floods and droughts all making regular appearances, often at most unexpected times of the year.

I very much like the short rhyme Geoffrey Lawes quotes in his new book 'The Victorian Beekeeping Revolution' taken from an early edition of the BBJ:

'First it hailed, then it blew,
And then it friz, then it snew
Then there came a shower of rain
Then it friz and snew again.'

We can do very little about the weather, indeed the vagaries of British weather make beekeeping more challenging. However, we can try to ensure that the bees are in tip top condition so that they are ready for any favourable opportunity that comes their way.

Let's hope that good weather, the strength of colonies and the availability of plentiful nectar and pollen sources are perfectly aligned in 2012.

John Phipps
Peloponnese, Greece
September 2011

I remember seeing in a 'culture' feature within a popular magazine the headline: "Have you got what it takes to be a WAG". To be honest, I didn't understand what the title meant until I scanned the text and soon realised by the lifestyles they were discussing, totally alien to anything which I have encountered, that WAG was an acronym for 'wives and girlfriends' of footballers.

HAVE YOU THE RIGHT QUALITIES AND DISPOSITION TO BE A BEE MASTER?

Well, let's slip into the more familiar world of beekeeping for a while and see how you measure up to the description of an ideal beekeeper as given by Revd Digges in his 'A Manual of Modern Beekeeping - Irish Bee Guide', first published in 1904.

What Constitutes "a Master of Bees."

"Therefore it is necessary, in order to manage bees, whether on the old principles or the new, that one should know how to stay "the beginning of strife," to subdue them to his will, and to bring them completely under control. Firmness, without aggression; gentleness, without fear; and a knowledge of their habits, tastes and fancies, are all required to constitute a master of bees. With such qualifications one can do with them as one pleases; can revolutionise their kingdom; depose their queen; regulate their enterprise; intercept their swarms; order the manner of their industry; deprive them of their stores; and, without provoking their anger , turn them again to peaceful labour. It is not a charm that may be worked by a privileged few. It is the application of knowledge to which all may attain readily."

SHOWING HONEY PRODUCTS

BY RON BROWN

It is probably true to say that almost every beekeeper in Britain has the opportunity to exhibit his produce at some local show within easy reach of his home. For instance, in Devon there are thirteen local branches of the County Beekeepers' Association, and each one of them stages a Honey Show at some time in the year. Every show has a section for novices, where your entry is competing only against other newcomers. Having gained confidence at this level, the next goal should be to exhibit at your County Show, where there will be many more entries and the standards are higher. The final objectives are the Royal Show at Stoneleigh in July and the National Honey Show in London, held for three days in October or November.

BBKA Show Rules
Even the smallest local show will produce a 'Schedule', setting out the various classes and quoting theconditions which have to be observed. These schedules are usually based on the Show Rules of the British Beekeepers' Association, Advisory Leaflet No. 22, obtainable from the Secretary, National Agricultural Centre, Stoneleigh, Warwickshire, CV8 2LZ. Among many points

covered are such basic ones as:-
(i) No exhibit may be entered in more than one class.
(ii) An exhibitor may make more than one entry in a class but shall not take more than one award in that class.
(iii) All honey and wax exhibited must be the natural produce of bees owned by the exhibitor, except
only for the candle and wax foundation-making classes.

Points the Judge will be looking for
Firstly - that the exhibit is of correct weight and in the right class, i.e. not too dark for the light honey class and so on. The judge will have a set of honey grading glasses (BSI No 1656) to check on this point.

Secondly - that the entry is free from such obvious faults as particles of foreign matter, seen when viewed in a strong light, rusty or discoloured lids, non-matching entries where two jars are specified, crystals or haze in a jar of 'clear' honey and so on. Normally any such entries are 'pushed back' and not given further consideration. Aroma and Flavour - are of paramount importance and a good judge will test for these with great care. The steward will loosen the cap but allow only the judge to remove it, so as to preserve the 'bouquet'. The flavour will be judged by tasting from a glass rod (one of several) carefully rinsed and dried after each tasting. Many competitors will gently warm their show honey to clear it of any traces of crystals; this is in order, but the occasional unscrupulous exhibitor may heat for rather longer to darken the honey a little, for example to get it into the 'dark' class. Any over-heating can readily be detected by smell, and by a slight flavour of caramel.

Clarity and Brightness - an exhibit of good colour and absolute clarity will have great appeal and often stand out among other entries. Some judges will 'pull forward' such an entry and 'push back' entries which are by contrast dull or even muddy looking. The surface of any honey should be completely free from any froth or scum.

Viscosity - this is tested by touching the surface of the honey with a glass rod and watching the liquid flow as the rod is lifted. A good honey is stiff and viscous whereas unripe honey is very 'runny' and more 'watery'.

Water Content - honey with a water content of more than 21 % (23% for heather or clover) may not legally be sold and most certainly would not win a prize in any show. A typical good specimen of honey could have a natural water content of 17% to 18%, and the lowest water content which I have personally ever measured has been 15%, as recorded by a Bellingham and Stanley refractometer (using Dr. Chataway's Tables). Most judges will not be using this instrument, but will make a fair assessment based
on long experience.

Granulated Honey

The judge will look first at the base, where any dark specks of foreign matter tend to settle and will immediately be noticed. The upper surface should be smooth, dry, uniform and of fine grain. A small pit at one side, indicating that the specimen has been judged before, is perfectly in order. Colour preferred is from a light lemon or gold to almost white, rather than a light khaki to brown. Patches of white 'frosting' on the side do not put the exhibit out of contention as they have no effect on flavour or aroma and arise naturally, but other things being equal a specimen with no 'frosting' woud be preferred. Granulated honey should not 'move' or flow noticeably when the jar is tilted for a while.

Frame of Honey for Extraction

The surface of the comb must be level and stand 'prouc' of the frame woodwork so that the uncapping knife may be used efficiently. The cells should be well filled and 100% capped, perhaps with just three or four open cells around the edges. When viewed from behind with a torch or bright light there should be a uniform colour with no dark patches indicating occasional cells of pollen. The wax cappings should be convex, either white or light yellow, with an absence of travel staining or weeping. There must be no tiny white tunnels visible just under the cappings (caused by larvae of Braula coeca, a small wingless insect sometimes found in beehives). Similarly there must be no trace of wax moth damage. The judge may test just one cell at the edge for quality of honey and absence of granulation. The cells should be uniform, i.e. all worker or all drone, with a slight preference for the larger drone cells, because from them the honey can be spun out more efficiently.

Section of Honey: Cut Comb

Few beekeepers today work for honey in the traditional wooden sections, but when successfully produced they command a high price. The comb should be as described in the previous paragraph, except that it will not come up to the level of the protective woodwork. Weight is not of paramount importance, so long as it is not less than 12 ounces, but preferably rather more. Much more honey today is sold as cut comb in plastic boxes, usually punched out of unwired new comb built on extra thin sheets of wax foundation, using a stainless steel Price's comb cutter. The judge will expect the cut comb to fill the plastic box generously with a minimum of liquid honey (better none at all)

Exhibitors should be aware that both sides of the comb may be inspected, and should not rely on the fact that only the better side is immediately visible. A comb with a small area uncapped below would be perfectly saleable but not a prize exhibit.

Chunk honey (cut comb in a jar surrounded by clear honey) makes an attractive exhibit, but few beekeepers seem to enter this class. The cut comb should be as large as possible and extend from top to bottom. The honey poured in after the comb is in position must be clear and similar in colour to that arising from the comb itself. Ragged edges, open cells with air bubbles, comb leaning over at an angle, would all cause marks to be lost at a show.

Heather Honey

This should have an even distribution of small bubbles, be firm so that the jar may be inverted with no visible flow, yet be clear and of a reddish amber colour with no granulation. It will have been obtained by pressing clean 'super combs in a honey press (borrowed from your local branch?). It is possible that unpressed honey, extracted by a Scandinavian machine using needles to agitate the honey in the cells and make it temporarily liquid, may be used. Heather honey is thixotropic, i.e. goes runny when stirred and then reverts to a jelly within few minutes, like some modem paints. As heather honey has a lower density, it is imperative that the jar be filled almost to lid level, or some judges will not even consider the entry, on the grounds that the weight is below that stipulated.

Beeswax

From rendered wax blocks to show standard exhibits involves enormous though rewarding work.

Judges usually prefer a colour between a pale straw or canary yellow and a light primrose or pale orange gold. Wax of a brighter orange has probably absorbed too much pigment from pollen or propolis. A very light wax might suggest that it has been bleached with acid or hydrogen peroxide, and many judges have a prejudice against such exhibits.

A good quality wax will have an aroma suggestive of the kind of honey from which it was elaborated by the bees. Wax from sugar fed bees will be lacking in aroma. A judge may gently warm the specimen by rubbing with the palm of his hand and smelling via hand cupped to nose. A freshly moulded wax cake will have more aroma than one made last year.

When beeswax solidifies from the liquid state it shrinks and loses over 8% of its volume. A wax cake which has cooled rapidly will have 'high shoulders' and often long, deep cracks, or at least a sunken, concave surface. Such an exhibit would be given very little consideration. A wax cake that has cooled much less rapidly (but still too quickly) may have a wavy surface, formed when the skin of solidified wax on the surface has had to bend slightly when the liquid wax below solidifies and takes up less space. At a local show, a wax cake good in other respects but with a slight ripple on its surface might gain an award, but not at County Show.

In general your wax cake should be clean, bright and translucent, with a complete absence of dark specks or any foreign matter. A judge may break off a tiny fragment from the edge, looking for a clean fracture with a fine granular texture: he may even chew it to confirm that it is neither too brittle, possibly from over-heating, or too gummy, also to appreciate the flavour and aroma of a natural product neither over- heated nor adulterated. The judge will also view the exhibit with a bright light shining behind it, to check on colour and absence of foreign matter.

Mead

Here a judge will be looking for brightness and clarity, and a light yellow/gold colour suggestive of the honey from which it was made. There must be a complete absence of any sediment, haze or bubbles indicating an on-going fermentation.

A small quantity poured into a thin glass, hand-warmed, should have a pleasing aroma or 'nose' and the taste should be crisp, clean and free from any hint of yeast, mustiness or 'off-flavour' acquired from metal or other contamination. As it lingers on the palate there can be a succession of flavours, all pleasant and without any slightly bitter after-taste which can sometimes downgrade an otherwise promising sample. A 'sweet' mead must contain some unfermented honey and have a fuller flavour than a 'dry' mead in which all the constituent sugars have been fermented to alcohol. Both classes must retain the bouquet and flavour of honey to some extent. No alcohol may be added to mead exhibited - a good judge will soon recognize a 'laced' sample.

Nowadays it is compulsory for mead to be exhibited in clear glass bottles (about 750 ml capacity) with shaped corks capable of being withdrawn without a corkscrew. The bases must be 'punted' i.e. convex inside to allow any sediment to be more easily seen. It should go without saying that the glass bottle be carefully chosen to be clear of any scratches, chipped edges or bubbles from manufacture.

Cakes and Biscuits

Obviously the size, weight, number of biscuits and recipe used must accord with the schedule. The outside of a cake should be well baked but not burnt. A slit in the top would indicate that the oven had been too hot. The cake should be of a well rounded shape with no sinking in the centre. When cut to the centre, it should reveal a close, soft texture with no patchiness or cavities. Any fruit in the recipe should be well distributed and not all at the bottom. The taste should be pleasing, with a good aroma and a distinct flavour of honey. Biscuits should be crisp rather than hard, of a reasonable thickness with an attractive colour and even surface.

Classes not specifically covered are:- creamed honey, wax candles, figures and flowers, observation hives, photographs, group exhibits and so on, but enough points have been made to give an insight into the judge's point of view.

Preparing Show Exhibits

Some regular exhibitors do quite well at times by just selecting the best samples of honey from their stocks. For the liquid honey classes, a few hours in a honey warming cabinet (temperature not exceeding 120°F (50°C) will clear any traces of granulation and brighten up most exhibits. If you have a fair stock of granulated honey then the best two may be worth staging as they are. However, if you really want to go for that silver cup or blue ribbon, preparation for the show has to start at extracting time in August or September.

Preparations.

The basic preparation for Honey Shows really starts at honey extracting time in August and September. Before extracting a single comb, have ready three empty boxes in which to place what may be your best honey, and methodically inspect all the frames in each super before you extract honey from one of them. Hold each up with a strong light shining through to check for absence of dark cells (pollen filled), or colour changes from comb centre to sides. Sometimes the central combs in a honey super will be darker (from the tail end of the spring flow) while the outer edges of the combs, worked on later by the bees, may contain light honey from clover or lime. If all combs are just extracted as they come to hand, you may end up with a very pleasant blend of summer honey but possibly all in the same class (medium), and no entries for light or dark honey. Also it can happen that a perfect comb, fit for exhibition in the 'frame for extraction' class, gets extracted and an opportunity missed. If good combs of light, medium and dark honey are put to one side in three separate boxes, these may be extracted later on by themselves.

Liquid Honey Classes.

First of all, check that any uncapped honey is at least 'ripe', i.e. that it does not run out like newly gathered nectar does when the frame is held horizontally and shaken. For normal use and for sale it is perfectly in order to extract and bottle from combs at least 75% sealed, but for show honey the extra density and viscosity to be expected from combs at least 90% sealed, may make the difference between award and no award. Any thin, unripe honey should be

14

spun out before uncapping and fed back to the bees. It is preferable to exhibit only honey from combs which have not been bred in. Many beekeepers practise one-and-a-half brood chamber management, and occasionally move shallows frames from brood chamber to honey super and vice versa. Under the centrifugal force of a fast rotating extractor, honey stored in the darker cells which have been bred in may well contain fragments of pupa skins and larval debris, and this may colour or flavour the honey to some extent.

A keen exhibitor will also scrape the wooden frames free of brace comb and propolis before uncapping, to prevent traces of darker wax and any foreign matter being dislodged in the extractor.

Uncapping. For some years I used an electrically heated uncapping knife, but came to realize that the temperature of the knife blade was hot enough to give a slightly caramelised flavour to the honey it contacted. Although this was but a tiny fraction of the whole, I could detect it myself, so clearly an experienced honey judge would also. When I adjusted the blade thermostat to a lower temperature, only just above wax melting point, then it ceased to be effective unless one worked very slowly, as it cooled by a few degrees and then dragged on the comb surface. Another practice suggested by some is to dip the uncapping knife into very hot water, but unless one wipes it completely dry each time, some water is added to the honey, reducing both density and viscosity. Many years ago I came back to using a very sharp, wavy edged 'Kitchen Devil' knife, working on combs still warm from the hive, or else gently warmed in a stack of supers over a 75 watt bulb in an empty brood box, with a 'bridge' of thin metal foil over the bulb to prevent a radiation hot spot melting an area of the nearest combs. The actual uncapping motion is similar to that of an expert chef carving a large ham, slicing neatly under the cappings to leave an exposed surface of open cells full of honey. A gentle to and fro sawing action is combined with a yawing motion, at the same time taking the knife along the length of the frame. It is suggested that the bulk of your crop be handled in the usual way, keeping back just enough frames to provide the very special show honey, and extracting these separately, perhaps in a small manual extractor.

Filtering. The secret of rapid and efficient filtration is to use warm honey and three successive layers of filters taking out coarse, small and very fine particles of wax etc. I do this very simply at home by using a standard stainless steel honey tank, in which the upper section has its own built-in filter of perforated metal. I tie a sheet of very fine denier nylon (such as that supplied to wine makers) below this, and place an ordinary kitchen colander in the upper chamber, resting on the metal filter. The colander holds back any large fragments of wax or the occasional splinter of wood which might otherwise choke the central filter, which in turn holds back small pieces, leaving the nylon to hold back only the tiniest particles. Used just by itself, the nylon would rapidly be choked by a layer of larger particles.

Bottling. It is best to wash a large number of glass honey jars at one time, and leave them inverted on wire trays in a warm room or conservatory, rather than drying them with a cloth. Although the general standard of new glassware is high, there are always some flaws, like the occasional bubble inside the actual glass, a small chip knocked out of the base, a thicker side or even a small pressure mark. So for show purposes, inspect your batch of six dozen washed jars very carefully and select several matched pairs of perfect specimens for your show honey.

Before bottling any honey, leave the honey tank for 24 hours, or at least over-night, in a warm place to allow any air bubbles or very small wax fragments to rise to the surface as froth. The glass jars themselves should be warmed, and held at an angle to the poured honey, so that it runs down the side of the tilted jar: in this way no air bubbles are trapped and carried into the jar. If you have a dog, especially a black one with a long wagging tail, keep him out of the room while bottling honey! I still remember once finding a single dog hair from our black Labrador in a jar of honey intended for showing. A fast wagging tail disperses thin hairs which can float unnoticed in the air but become very obvious in a jar of light honey. After bottling four jars (to give a choice) I would recommend running the remainder of that specially selected honey into a scrupulously clean glass vessel, stoppered and labelled for future show use. Ex-sweet jars (14 lbs) or household storage jars (screw topped) of 7 lbs capacity have been found useful in this respect. For checking the colour of your exhibits as to correct class for entry purposes, a really keen exhibitor should use a set of the official honey grading glasses (BSI No. 1656) referred to in the previous article.

Granulated Honey. Most honies will granulate after a few months, notable exceptions being pure heather honey and fuchsia. Some (like oil seed rape) will granulate within hours, others within a week or two but most not for several weeks. In order to get very fine and even granulation it is best to store the honey in jars in a cellar or cool spot where there will not be any rapid temperature changes. Although a temperature of 14°C (57°C) is regarded as best. I have not noticed much difference in the range (8 - 16°F). It is important that honey intended to granulate for showing is neither in a draught nor exposed to light from a window. If one side of the jar be colder than the other, then 'frosting' is much more likely. Since medium or darker honies granulated to khaki or brown set honey (not favoured by most judges), it is important to start with a light honey, which will give at least a creamy yellow or even golden colour when granulated. A 'water white' liquid honey (e.g.

from oil seed rape) will set to a flat, white colour, looking almost like lard. Nothing wrong with this, but most judges prefer more colour. Honey filtered and bottled straight from the extractor tends to have more air dissolved in it (from the whirling and violent air currents around the rotating frames). Even after settling for 24 hours much of the dissolved air remains, but comes out on granulation, whether in a 28 lbs tin or a jar. On re-heating to liquify before bottling, the second granulation usually does not show 'frosting' and has less of a thin 'scum' of minute bubbles on the surface. Incidentally, the actual surface of a jar of naturally granulated honey may be slightly moist but should not be wet; sometimes the skilled use of a disc of absorbent paper (blotting or filter) can remove the last trace of wetness.

Frame of Honey for Extraction. Although the woodwork of the frame does not have to be new, it must be scrupulously clean and free from stains. Careful scraping with the small blade of a penknife can achieve this, but new frames with freshly drawn combs probably have a slight advantage.

A new frame rubbed with a slight smear of medicinal paraffin (liquid paraffin) or vaseline, will be less likely to acquire propolis deposits or stains.

Bees in a hurry during a strong honey flow will sometimes draw some large (drone size) honey cells even on worker comb or foundation, and a mixture of the two can lose some credit. A new frame fitted with a sheet of drone foundation will have a uniform cell pattern. Other advantages are that pollen is much less likely to be stored in drone cells, and also honey is more easily and completely spun out of drone cells in an extractor.

From a health point of view, a few cells of pollen in a honeycomb should be a bonus, but judges (and most customers) do not see it as such. In this connection it should be remembered that the central three or four combs in the first super above the queen excluder are more likely to have pollen stored in them.

Frames of honey for extraction should be wired to strengthen the comb against centrifugal forces, and a careful judge will look for this when shining a torch through. The one exception would be a frame of heather honey, normally extracted by pressing and so not needing any wire for support. The actual comb surface should be as flat and regular as possible; some are naturally built that way but it can help to have thin dividers (as with sections). Some books suggest thin plywood, but much better are the smooth, thinner sheets of a more modem material, Formica, Wearite or some such laminate (as used on kitchen surfaces or table tops). This can be cut into remarkably rigid sheets, to fit between frames without adding any appreciable bulk.

Beeswax.
Casting a really good cake of exhibition wax is one of the most difficult (and exasperating) tasks. The best wax is usually from cell cappings, and

so preparation starts at extracting time, when it is important first to scrape frames clear of propolis and burr comb before capping, also to avoid cutting too deep into cells so as to include older cell walls. Cappings are freshly made by the bees each season, but cells may endure for 20 years in well kept honey frames, and will darken in colour after this time.

Some comb surfaces will be whiter than others; in general terms the shorter the time in the hive, the whiter the wax.

As well as cappings, pieces of virgin comb as sometimes built down into an empty space are obviously suitable. After uncapping several supers of chosen combs, the cappings should be drained overnight, carefully washed in rain water and spread out on a white cloth to dry, in a warm room. At this stage pick out by hand any darker fragments or obvious impurities which have somehow got in, and check that you have enough (say 10 to 12 ozs, about 300g), assuming that an 8oz cake is in the schedule. If you have only one or two hives, you will not be able to be so choosy about the wax, and will have to use whatever you can muster from all sources.

The wax can be melted in a Pyrex jug standing on a wire triangle in a pan of hot water over a very low heat. To reach National Honey Show standard the wax must be filtered through a filter paper (coffee or Whatmans No. 1 obtained from a chemist or school lab.), but the pores of filter paper are so small that one has to filter first through lint (fluffy side up) to prevent tiny impurities from blocking the pores.

The chosen mould (Pyrex or similar domestic ovenware) should be carefully washed, dried and then polished with the merest trace of detergent on a dry linen cloth; after this, on no account allow a finger to touch the inside surface of the mould. Together with the final filter and jug of liquid wax the mould should be warmed to about 80°C (180°F) in the oven, before the pouring, and any air bubbles afterwards removed with a needle point. The oven should be fitted with a tray of two or three dry bricks on the top shelf, to hold the heat and maintain the temperature of the upper wax surface.

Check that the mould rests on a perfectly level surface in the oven.

After pouring the wax to a pre-determined level, place a sheet of glass over the mould. It is best to do all this last thing at night, and to go to bed after closing the oven door and switching off the oven. This avoids accidental vibrations from other people working in the kitchen, also the temptation of looking in from time to time. Next morning lift out the mould and invert it over a towel on a kitchen working surface. If the wax fails to come out after a gentle tap, cool in the fridge for a couple of hours and try again, or place the mould plus wax (right way up) in a bowl of cold water, when the wax should float up, to be carefully dried with a smooth towel. A gentle polish with a dry thumb or piece of well-worn silk should give the final touch. For a fuller description one can refer to a specialised text in a library, ('Beeswax', published by B.B.N.O).

18

It is appreciated that several items have not been covered, for example honey cakes and biscuits, heather honey, wax candles, mead, cut combs and sections. Some of these topics have been covered in previous 'Home Farm' articles, for example mead in issue No. 66, heather honey in issue No. 41, but it is hoped that the examples described will give some idea of the approach to exhibition in Honey Shows, and that readers will be encouraged to enter in their local and county shows, where there are special classes for 'beginners', and later on at the Royal and the National, where their exibits will be seen by many thousands of people, even by Royalty!

The National Honey Show presents annually a three day show of the best of the products of the honeybee, with additional classes for kindred interests and skills, including school bee-keeping, a lecture programme and a display of the latest and finest bee-keeping equipment on the market today.

It attracts entries and beekeepers from all over these Isles, and a number of leading organisations hold meetings during the Show.

From: Showing honey products (No.9) by Ron Brown, A NATIONAL HONEY SHOW PUBLICATION, reproduced by permission of David Smart, Chairman, NHS

NB. Apart from wishing to provide interest and pleasure for Beekeepers, the National Honey Show has the serious aim of raising the standards of production of honey and all other bee-produce. With this objective in view, leading authorities have been invited to write for our Schedules on a number of subjects and their work is here available for more general distribution. We wish to thank all our contributors; they are leading exponents of their skills. We have, however, to make it clear that the advice which they give is their own individual method. We feel sure that they would be the first to encourage new alternative ways of preparation with a view to continual advancement and progress within the Craft.

Hon. General Secretary
NATIONAL HONEY SHOW

Ragwort spp.

BEEKEEPERS BEES POISONING FARMERS?

BILL CLARKE

MAGOG HILLS, CAMBRIDGE

My wife, and her sister, have always lived what they believe to be a healthy life-style; the fact that they have a beekeeping husband/brother-in-law who passes over gifts of honey and mead, they have always looked on as a bonus - until now!

Sister-in-law's husband rang me up at the end of June: "Bill, I have just read a piece in 'The Lady' magazine by Robin Page; he says that some honey is poisonous!" And almost accusingly he asked, "Did you know this?" I leapt to my own defence, rubbishing farmer and conservationist Robin Page's notion - who I happen to have met on a few occasions - and asked for a copy of the article to be posted to me.

My memory got up to speed as I stepped over to my books: many years ago whilst passing by an unusual lime tree, I was intrigued to notice that the grass growing beneath was extra green in a circle matching the spread of the branches, and surmised that the honeydew dripping down had fertilised it. However, on closer inspection I discovered a veritable carpet of the rotted remains of bees, and wondered by what quirk of nature such a tree could exist. Next, in the mid eighties, I noticed that Cambridge City workers had planted two by the roadside. I now know they are the Lime trees (*Tilia petiolaris*), and being fairly near to my home, have occasionally visited them at flowering time. I can report that there are only a few dead bees in a normal season, but they lie in their hundreds beneath the trees in a dry one - when I am sorely tempted to take my axe to them. I deemed it was high time that I discovered what toxic element exists in their pollen or nectar. The 'Book of Honey' by Eva Crane seemed a good place to start, and on pages 52 to 53 she came up trumps. Not only a list of the contents in the nectar - it contains unusual sugars not toxins - but a full technical description of why the bees are unable to digest some of the sugar, ending up with them being paralysed when there is a lower water content.

Also on page 52, I found: "A few honeys, and the nectar or honeydew they are derived from, are toxic to man." Followed by the story of a famous incident from 400 BC, when Xenophon wrote of his Grecian Army ascending a mountain in order to camp among a number of villages, well stocked with food. "There were also large numbers of beehives, and all the soldiers who ate the honey went off their heads and suffered from vomiting and diarrhoea and were unable to stand upright. Those who had eaten a little behaved as though drunk, and those who had eaten a lot were like mad people." It was not until the third and fourth day after partaking of the honey that a very weakened army was back on its feet!

Eva believed that the nectar had originated from *Rhododendron ponticum* - most other known toxic honeys are from members of this Ericaceae family - and that besides toxicity in honey being very rare, in most cases it dissipates as the honey ripens, leading her to suspect that the Greek soldiers took unripe honey direct from the hives. I wondered too, if soil and/or warmer climes could have a bearing on the toxicity, however, another author, after quoting similar stories about these plants abroad, wrote that he had himself obtained honey from rhododendrons growing in Cobham, Kent, and that, ". . no person who partook of a spoonful could persuade it to stay put for more than a quarter of an hour, but this emetic effect was the only discomfiture experienced."

There are very few pollens and nectars known to be really 'poisonous' - one or two examples are in flowers that are not visited by bees - but one such that bees will visit, is Yellow jessamine (*Gelsemium sempervirons*) - at least by killing the bees, it means that the honey should not arrive on the human table. The usual human poisoning from this plant - which grows wild in America - is because children have sucked the nectar from the sweet smelling flowers. We beekeepers have often grumbled about careless spraying in the past, but perhaps we should be paying more attention to what's being planted, for both the afore mentioned shrubs - and just about all the other members of the large families involved, are planted in gardens to provide embellishment or scent. The Mountain laurel or Calico bush (*Kalmia latifolia*) - another popular garden shrub - is listed as being among the nine plants suspected of being most responsible for bee deaths in America. (I was very surprised to see black nightshade - *Solanum nigrum* - in that list, for black nightshade is a very common weed in Britain, especially on light sandy soils).

Thankfully - in Britain - such shrubs in range of our beehives are few in number; even so, one in full flower when there is little other bee forage, could presumably cause a problem. Happily most nectars and pollens from toxic plants have little or no effect on the bees or their brood - it is not very sensible for a plant to poison it's pollinators - and fewer still affect the human honey imbiber. But I do wonder if every gardener read my books regarding plant poisons, whether they might consign half their plants to a bonfire; for few would dare to keep such as their Oleander one hour longer than necessary, after reading: "All parts of this plant are highly toxic. Eating a single leaf or even meat skewered during cooking by oleander has been recorded as deadly."

The cutting from, 'The Lady', entitled, LIFE ON THE FARM, duly arrived with me. Adorned by a small photo of Oxford ragwort (*Senecio squalidus*), Robin explains ragwort's toxicity to farm animals by damaging the liver - dangerous to cattle and more so to horses, and surmises that sheep, rabbits and wild deer seem to be able to cope with it, and is amazed that the Cinnabar moth caterpillars survive on it as their main food plant. He quite rightly deplores the fact that little now seems to be done to stop the spread of such a toxic weed; pointing out that it is in fact illegal to allow it to grow on your land. The fact that he never eats honey from known Ragwort infested areas, shows he believes honey produced from Ragwort is toxic, and he announces his astonishment that the Food Standards Agency confirmed that no research has been done on the subject.

Should beekeepers be worried? A beekeeping author writing in the late 1940s, says of ragwort: ". . produces a large quantity of honey, so that late supers often contain a lot of it in some districts. It is a rich, golden colour, but its taste is positively nauseous," but if it is allowed to mature, "it loses much of its nastiness." And another in 1976 writes, ". . it is bright yellow and has so offensive an odour that when first extracted it is completely unpalatable. Once granulated however, the smell is lost and the honey is quite good." After a near neighbour in 1986 allowed a field to become overrun with Ragwort, I can corroborate that these beekeepers are correct in all aspects, and I assume, due to their phrasing, that they both consumed some. Due to the fact that I ate a jar or two of it too - and that I am writing this so many years later - I can confirm that it is not truly toxic! A further beekeeping author in the 90s, finds ragwort honey adds a bit of interest, and finishes with, "A recent MAFF survey to assess levels of PAs in UK honey produced by bees with access to ragwort stated that there was no cause for alarm." In 2007, an 'Environment' section within a Beekeeping magazine, commences: Yellow Peril? And complains about an OTT article about ragwort in the Daily Mail, which seems to have emphasised that the countryside was being taken over by ragwort - killing thousands of horses each year and giving liver cirrhosis to humans. The author mentions much of what is in this article, but also points out the very relevant benefit to 177 invertebrates that feed on ragwort nectar and the 77 species of insect-herbivores that have been recorded on the plant, ending with, "there is no evidence to suggest that it is likely to become a problem within beekeeping."

Because of my farming connections, I have always believed it was my duty to destroy all ragwort plants, in fact, as was pointed out in the above magazine article, there is a 'Ragwort Control Act', made law in 2003. An environmentalist, writing in a national magazine around that time, advised dressing up in full body armour and face mask before tackling ragwort, yet I have pulled up hundreds of plants bare handed - still do. Other environmentalists have grumbled at me for trashing the food plants of the Cinnabar moths offspring - however, I point out that these insects also use Groundsel (*Senecio vulgaris*) so my conscience is clear. Various Finches love pecking at groundsel, in fact a bunch of it was a permanent feature in my grandmother's canary cage, which makes me wonder if it is the least toxic member of the family. All birds avoid eating the Cinnabar caterpillars, proof enough that the toxins are present in their bodies too.

I believe ragwort is most probably toxic to most of the animal kingdom - including man - if it is eaten either green and sappy, or dead and dried. It takes time for the toxicity to build up in the liver, and therein lies the reason for the erroneous thinking that horses are more susceptible than smaller animals. All grazing animals seem to dislike the pungent taste, but will ingest some leaves - either by design or accident - whilst grazing close to the plants; and perhaps by extreme hunger. The toxins build up in those animals livers over years, and the long-lived horse is the most likely to arrive at a lethal dose when eating small regular amounts, whilst the short lived sheep and rabbit may not reach that threshold - I wonder if Robin worries about eating lambs livers from ragwort areas? Most horse fatalities are caused by feeding hay containing ragwort. Because the pungency is not so evident in the dried plants, the animals don't try to avoid it, the effect - added to any build up already present in their livers - will be quite rapid; even with the small animals eating it.

Does this point to the fact that the even longer living humans, could die because of toxic build up in the liver, caused by eating ragwort honey? Well, there are variables working in our favour. First, ragwort usually flowers at the end of the main honey flow season, so many beekeepers leave it in the hives for winter feed. Second, in seasons like 2011, when it flowers early, it will be watered down with all the other nectars that are being collected, and if it does give a honey flow separate from other flowers, the horrible taste and vivid yellow of the honey is usually enough to put most beekeepers off, and even if they only find out after they have harvested it, it is fed back to the bees later. Third, the well known enzyme action and antibacterial build up in mature honey seems to be very effective in dealing with this particular toxin, and I believe puts an end to the problem.

The caution I would give to fellow beekeepers, is do not make a habit of eating fresh ragwort honey - better to use it for winter feed - and encourage your horse-keeping neighbours to destroy their plants, after all it is in their own interests. And to all folk, who like me eat honey, don't worry about enjoying the occasional extra golden honey. Don't bulk buy extra strong tasting, liquid, and very yellow honey - just in case!

References: BEE-KEEPING NEW AND OLD, W Herrod-Hempsall, 1930s. The Hive and the Honey Bee, R A Grout, 1954. BEES, FLOWERS and FRUIT, Herbert Mace, late 40s early 50s. Guide to BEES and HONEY, Ted Hooper, 1976. A Book of Honey, Eva Crane, 1980. Practical Beekeeping, Clive de Bruyn, 1997. The Beekeepers Quarterly', an article by Geoff Hopkinson NDB, in Number 89 2007. Deadly Harvest, John Kingsbury, 1965. Dangerous Plants, John Tampion, 1977.

EDITOR"S NOTE
Injurious weeds, invasive and alien plants.
Legal status

Injurious weeds - five weeds are classified under the Weeds Act 1959: common ragwort (*Senecio jacobaea*), spear thistle (*Cirsium vulgare*), creeping or field thistle (*Cirsium arvense*), broad-leaved dock (*Rumex obtusifolius*) and curled dock (*Rumex crispus*). It is not an offence to have these weeds growing on your land and species such as ragwort have significant conservation benefits. However they must not be allowed to spread to agricultural land, particularly grazing areas or land which is used to produce conserved forage. Enforcement notices can be issued following complaints requiring landowners to take action to prevent the spread of these weeds.

Invasive weeds - include Himalayan Balsam an excellent late season forage plant for honeybees though causing enormous problems in the Norfolk Broads, giant hogweed a skin irritant in humans, but also a good honey plant, and Japanese Knotweed which can destroy pavements and river banks due to its quick growth

Alien plants - In May 2008 the GB Strategy for invasive non-native species (INNS) was launched by English Nature. One of the key elements of the strategy was a recognition of the need to prevent the introduction and/ or spread of potentially invasive non-native species. Determining which species will become invasive is notoriously difficult, the best predictor being evidence of invasiveness elsewhere. To assist in the prioritisation and targeting of prevention work, Natural England sought a horizon-scanning exercise to identify non-native plants that are most likely to become invasive in Great Britain in the future.

Many of the plants which were already or likely to be a problem are very good sources of pollen for bees and other pollinating insects. The data basis created by English Nature's Horizon Scanning plan categorised the plants according to their rank from critical to low risk. Plants of value to beekeepers are:

Critical List
Tree of Heaven (*Ailanthus altissima*), Butterfly Bush (*Buddleia davidii*), many species of Cotoneaster, Garden Privet (*Ligustrum ovalifolium*), Bay (*Laurus nobilis*), Japanese Honeysuckle (*Lonicera japonica*), Giant Butterbur (*Petasites japonicus*), Firethorn (*Pyracantha spp*) False Acacia (*Robinia psuedoacacia*)

Urgent List
Snowberry (*Symphoricarpos microphyllus x orbicularis*), Tree Lupin (*Lupinus arboreus*), Red Hot Poker (*Kniphofia uvaria* & *K x praecox*), Spanish Gorse (*Genista hispanica*), Orange Ball Tree (*Buddleia globosa*), Spotted Laurel (*Aucuba japonica*) and Italian Alder (*Alnus cordata*).

A copy of the whole list of plants and their status can be downloaded from English Nature's website: **www.naturalengland.org.uk**

ITALIAN BEES - THE GOLDEN WONDER? A short history of the early importation of Italian Queens into Engand and the USA.

by John Phipps

Rev L L Langstroth says of the Italian bees :
"They gather more than twice as much honey in the same localities, in the same time, as the swarms of native bees."

The first bees I ever kept were a strain of pure Italians from E H Taylor of Welwyn Garden City. The bees arrived as a six frame nucleus just a few weeks after I had completed a three-day beekeeping course there by Messrs Haynes and Patterson.

Undeniably, the bees were gentle and easy to handle; they drew out the combs quickly and by August gave me almost a full super of honey. For a beginner they were ideal. I didn't receive one sting in the first few months and finding the golden tan-coloured queen was never difficult.

However, problems did emerge in the following year when a second generation of bees were raised by making splits. These bees were totally unrecognisable from the bees of the previous year both in colour (not a problem) and behaviour (a real problem which had to be contended with). They were aggressive, ankle-stinging followers, bees which stung me so badly on one occasion that I had to seek medical aid due to an adverse reaction to their stings; so much so in fact that I thought that this might have been the end of my beekeeping days.

Fortunately, I have suffered no adverse reaction to bee stings since that one occasion forty years ago, despite having had thousands of stings, but it did make me aware of the fact that imported queens were okay, as long as you intended to keep buying in pure bred queens from the importer. Okay, for oneself, I should have said, for the crossing of local newly-emerged queens mated with my Italian drones would undoubtedly have caused problems for other beekeepers in my area.

It was really only when I met Beowulf Cooper that I began to realise more fully the impact that foreign races had on local strains of bees, and since that time I have tried to select queen rearing material from colonies which had good breeding potential as seen on the list of the virtuous characteristics laid down by BIBBA.

Despite the best efforts of Beowulf and his organisation, it was obvious that it was going to be an uphill struggle for the campaign, for that is what it seemed at the time, to be successful.

I remember Cecil Tonsley giving a lecture on the good qualities of Italian bees which was immediately followed by Beowulf taking over the platform to talk about the native Black. Neither of the speakers referred to each other; they could have been from separate planets, but as often is the case, the audience must have been totally perplexed as to whom they should believe. This is frequently the case when two experts with conflicting opinions deliver their lectures in the same afternoon.

However, this is not an article which is meant to be disparaging towards Italian bees; after all, I have kept pure strains and enjoyed them. Indeed, the Italian bee is the most prominent bee in commercial apiaries around the world. So my question is, fundamentally, why has it become so popular?

According to one writer, though I forget his name, the importation of Italian bees into England, to him, was second only to Langstroth's utilisation of the bee space in his hives, as regards milestones in the history of beekeeping.

The First Imports of Italian Queens.
The first Italian bees which reached England (1859) and the USA (1860) were imported, respectively, by Woodbury and Neighbour, and the US government. H M Fraser in his book 'History of Beekeeping in Britain' relates that the 'Italian' bees originally came from the Tessin region of Switzerland, the plains of which slope into Italy'.

Samuel Simmins
One of the biggest proponents of Italian bees (or Ligurians as he called them) was Samuel Simmins in the latter part of the 19th century. His book, 'A Modern Bee Farm' was printed by the thousands and is still worthy of a close read even today. Within his book he lists the qualities of most of the bee races and whilst he favoured, bred, and sold hundreds of Italian queens, he is fair in his assessment of them, though it's true that many of

his followers particularly liked their golden colours (F W Sladen used their colour as a very important selling point for his Italian Queens). At the time of his writing the 1904 revised edition of his book he says that 'there is perhaps hardly a district where the native bees have not to some extent . . . . received some benefit of the infusion of fresh blood.' He goes on to say that whilst old fashioned beekeepers considered the Italians to be inferior to native bees, the influence of the Italian was so strong that after each cross the Italian colouring gradually disappeared and the 'blacks' which many beekeepers declared to be better were in fact Italians in disguise - something he found quite amusing.

(A) Advantages (B) Disadvantages of Italian Bees (in contrast to British Blacks):

(A) More prolific; gather more honey; can reach deeper nectaries; continue to forage well into autumn; draw out foundation well even late in the season; and more gentle.

(B) Stored honey in comb not so good; not such good comb builders (despite reference to foundation drawing above!); reluctant to enter supers; produce only a few queen cells so no good for queen rearing.

Summary - good all round bee; hybrids will be energetic workers but with very bad tempers.

Henry Alley
In his book 'The Beekeeper's Handbook, or Twenty-Two Years Experience in Queen Rearing' (1), Alley quotes Dzierzon as being the person who should be credited for popularising the Italian bee. Aided by the Austrian agricultural society of Vienna, Dzierzon imported the first Italian bees into Austria; 'and after throughly testing them, pronounced them superior in every respect to the native, as they swarmed earlier, were more industrious and hence better honey gatherers, more gentle and yet more courageous and active in self

defence and far more beautiful'. So, once again we get a strong hint that beekeepers were attracted by the cosmetic appearance of the race and on the down side, but cleverly put as a positive trait, the bees could be very bad tempered.

Alley claims that the first live Italian queens reached the USA in 1859 were imported by Messrs Wagner, Colvin and Mahan and goes on to say that these importations led to the 'bee fever' which struck America 'both as a science and a remunerative vocation'.

However, after a quarter of a century Alley acknowledged that the Italian bees in the USA, due most likely to hybridisation, were no longer a distinct race, but an American Italian strain 'superior in every respect to any ever imported from Italy'. Alley is therefore saying much the same as Simmins, that the Italians were better for all purposes once they had been crossed with the local bees.

Mrs Lizzie E Cotton, authoress of 'Beekeeping for Profit', 3rd Edition, Maine, USA, 1891.

MRS. LIZZIE E. COTTON.

Some of my friends claim that the honey collected by the Italian is of better flavor, and a nicer quality generally, than that collected by the common bees; and this may be the case in some localities where there are certain varieties of flowers accessible to the Italians, but not accessible to the natives, the latter being smaller. Yet in my location I see no difference in the quality of the honey collected by the two varieties, but a great difference in favor of the Italians, in the quantity collected.

I will furnish six full swarms of Italian Bees, each in Controllable Hive; the brood section (six moveable comb frames) filled with comb, honey, eggs and hatching brood well supplied with bees ; a healthy prolific queen; everything ready for work; full swarms, strong and healthy ; first class in every respect, with full set of boxes (the two sizes) in place on the hive each box containing comb ready for the bees to fill with honey feeder on each ready for feeding. I will furnish the six swarms as described, for One Hundred Dollars. I will furnish one swarm of Italian Bees in Controllable Hive with boxes, feeder and all fixtures required for Twenty Dollars.

Spring is the best time to commence Bee Keeping on my plan. No one need be prevented from obtaining these bees no matter how great the distance they reside from me.

I guarantee safe delivery at any express office.

The BBJ

A page featuring early issues of the BBJ from Geoffrey Lawes' delightful and authoritative new book 'The Victorian Beekeeping Revolution'.

The
Victorian Beekeeping
Revolution

Not surprisingly, the case for or against Italian bees featured prominently in the pages of the British Bee Journal which was founded in 1873, 14 years after the first introduction of Italian bees into England. By this time beekeepers were quite familiar with these imports and the most notable writers of the time tended to give them almost unreserved support, though several, of course, had a vested interest in their sales (This seemed to be the case well into the later years of the BBJ; I remember Beowulf Cooper saying in his usual matter-of-fact way that the BBJ was built on, and continued to function by, advertising revenue from the sellers of imported queens).

Whilst I have no back copies of the journal to sift through, fortunately Geoffrey Lawes has recently written 'The Victorian Beekeeping Revolution' (2) with much of the material gleaned from the BBJ since its inception. Regarding Ligurian (Italian) bees, in the first Vol of the BBJ in March, we learn that breeding bees was thwart with diffculties: Lawes writes, quoting from the BBJ, 'The immediate challenge was to keep control of the progeny of Ligurians "the superior qualities of which are acknowledged by all beekeepers" and to prevent the "highborn and beautiful queen'" from "marrying beneath her". The beekeeper who finds that she has produced undesirable hybrids "in disgust at his disappointment, simply pinches her head off". As Lawes says, ' "Ligurianising" was proving a vexatious process which often ended in tears. Later on this is reiterated when Lawes relates that the BBJ had many enquiries from beekeepers 'who needed to know the manipulations needed to follow the fashion for replacing black bees with Ligurians'. Lawes also gleans that Ligurian queens which were selling for 30 shillings in 1964 were available in 1874 from the BBJ office for only seven shillings and sixpence; by then they were obviously so numerous and easily available that beekeepers were able to obtain them at the much lower price. By the 1890s we hear that whilst Ligurian bees continued to be popular, other beekeepers began to look for more exotic bees, especially those from Cyprus.

Italian Bees: Original Source Material

1. The New England Farmer, Volume 12. September 1860

During the early part of last year the Commissioner of Patents at Washington authorized Mr. S. B. Parsons, of Long Island, N. Y., to proceed to Italy, and inquire into the habits of Italian bees, and if, upon investigation, he found them possessing qualities of value which American native bees did not possess, to procure a certain number of swarms and send them to the Patent Office.

He entered upon the duties assigned him, and arrived in the country of the Italian Lakes in April, 1859. After wandering about among the hills of that delightful region for some months, his researches were arrested by the approach of hostile armies, and he was not able to resume them until the following September, when he met an intelligent Bavarian who had established himself in the Grisons, and had devoted himself to the culture of pure Italian bees.

The result of his researches convinced him that these bees possessed qualities superior to those of our own, and he ordered for the Department to the full amount which he was authorized to expend, and directed them to be sent by the Arago on the 18th of October from Havre, but by some unaccountable delay they were not shipped until December 28th, from Genoa.

In his investigations, Mr. Parsons says he came to the following conclusions in relation to the Italian bees:

1. That they will endure the cold better than ours.
2. That they swarm twice as often.
3. That they are abundantly more prolific.
4. That the working bees begin to forage earlier, and are more industrious.
5. That they are less apt to sting, and may be easily tamed by kind treatment.
6. That the queen may be so educated as to lay her eggs in any hive in which she is placed, while the bees of such a hive, deprived of their own queen, will readily receive her.
7. That its proboscis is longer, and it can reach the depths of flowers which are entirely beyond the efforts of the common bee.
8. That a young queen, once impregnated, will continue fertile during her life—from four to seven years. This quality will insure pure broods, till the whole country is fllled with them.
9. That they are far more brave and active than the common bee; will fight with great fierceness, and are more effectually at keeping the moth out of the hive.

Having read the statement of Mr. Parsons, and learning that Mr. Brackett, of Winchester, in this State, a gentleman who has gained some celebrity as a 'skillful cultivator of several varieties of grapes', had introduced the Italian bee into his colonies, we visited his place a few days since, and examined both bees and grapes for ourselves. In the midst of his delightful retreat, surrounded on all sides but the south by the natural forest, he nestles on the hillside with his pleasant family, his forcing houses, grapes, and other plants, and his twenty odd swarms of bees! He is full of zeal in regard to them all,—and that zeal is so admirably tempered with knowledge, that one cannot fail to gather valuable suggestions upon any of his favorite topics. Mr. Brackett was early called into consultation with Mr. Parsons, and one or two other distinguished apiarians, in regard to the course to be pursued with the Italian bees, and as a part of the policy he has introduced eight pure queens into his colonies, having first by a most ingenious device driven all the drones, or males, of the common bee from his hives. The queen of the common bee and the drone brood being taken away, and a new Italian queen introduced, the natural work was at once entered upon of forming new queen and brood cells, so that the eggs deposited by the new queen would produce the pure Italian bee!

From the experience thus far gained, Mr. Brackett is inclined to confirm the statements made by Mr. Parsons. He thinks their merits have not been overrated, and states that they are more easily managed, and less sensitive to cold than our bees.

From a little work by H. C. Hermann, the Bavarian referred to above, we learn that the yellow, Italian bee is a mountain insect; it is found between two mountain chains, to the right and left of Lombardy and the Rhetian Alps, and comprises the whole territory of Tessir, Veltlin and South Graubunden. It thrives up to the height of 4500 feet above the level of the sea, and appears to prefer the northern clime to the warmer, for in the south of Italy it is not found.

It differs from our common black bee in its longer, slender form, and light chrome-yellow color, with brimstone-colored wings, and two orangered girths, each one-sixth of an inch wide. Working bees as well as drones have this mark. The drones are further distinguished by the girths being scolloped, like the spotted water-serpent, and attain an astonishing size; almost half as corpulent again as the black drones. The queen has the same marks as the working bees, but much more conspicuous, and lighter; she is much larger than the black queen, and easy to be singled out of the swarm on account of her remarkable bodily size and light color.

We engaged with Mr. Brackett in some manipulations, such as taking out the queen bee and a drone or two for examination, and peeping into some of the nuclei which he is forming.

2. American Agriculturist, Volume 19. August 1860
Inaugurating a Queen Bee

The incidents attending the inauguration of a Queen among bees, are less ceremonious, perhaps, than a similar transaction among men, yet to the observing naturalist they are full of interest. An account of one of these events, happening the present season, was described in a private letter, recently received by Samuel B. Parsons, and it interested us so much, that we solicited the privilege of making the extract below. Mr. J. H. Pierce of Montgomery County, Ohio, received an Italian Queen bee from Mr. Parsons, and Mr. Langstroth happening to be in the neighborhood, was requested to undertake the ceremony of inaugurating the new-comer as royal mistress over a native stock. It will be seen, that the republican tribe did not at first submit quietly to the usurpation.

"....He (Mr. L.) first took away the Queen from a colony, driving off the bees that followed her, and when they had become uneasy and anxious from the loss of their Queen, he presented the new Queen at the entrance of the hive, in which were the bees which had adhered to the comb, and those that had returned from abroad. She entered immediately, but was instantly surrounded and enclosed by a knot of bees, and uttered a shriek of alarm, which caused Mr. Langstroth to disperse the bees and catch her, for fear she would be smothered. He then introduced her in the wire cage, in which she had been sent, and hung her in the hive, permitting the whole swarm to return. He left her in this way perhaps half an hour, and as they appeared to be feeding her, then released her among the bees, who appeared to be now more willing to receive her. This was about 12 o'clock. After dinner, at 3, Mr. Langstroth started home.

Mr. Rossel, the beekeeper, after this went to the hive, took off the honey-board, and found the Queen on the bottom of the hive, running as fast as possible, the bees pursuing her, and she squeaking. She ran out in front and took wing, but as she rose above his head, he fortunately caught her, and clipped her wings. He then sprinkled the hive with peppermint water, and as the bees in a few moments appeared quiet, gave them the Queen again, and they received her very peaceably. The next morning, he examined the hive, and found her upon the comb "all right." Mr. Pierce writes further :

"We now attribute the trouble to the fact of Mr. Langstroth's cleansing some wax from his fingers with turpentine, just before he handled the Queen, and they retained the scent, although he washed them afterwards in clear water. We have found, if bees are robbing a hive, and the owners are dispirited, that a little whiskey, sprinkled upon the floor of the hive, so excites and enrages them, that they at once fight furiously, and kill every robber they can lay hold of. The turpentine doubtless has the same effect, and the queen being scented with it, was very offensive to the bees. I have entered into this detail, presuming you will be interested in our method and success, and also that you may have additional proof of the delicacy of the bees' olfactories, and the danger of offending them in this regard"

Why do Italian Bees Remain so Popular?

It is undoubtedly the case that various strains of Italian bees are the mainstay of commercial beekeeping throughout the world. So why have they remained so popular and why have beekeepers kept faithful to bees of Italian origin?

Perhaps the last word should go to R O B Manley who is renown for his success in commercial beekeeping and whose books have been an inspiration to would-be commercial beekeepers.

In 'Honey Farming' (3) - first published in 1946 - he writes: 'Italians and their crosses for me every time. You know, whether we like it or not, we

Italian bees remain the most commercially popular type of bee in the world.

have most of us to use cross-bred bees, and the Italian crosses are the best crosses in my opinion. My counsel is to aim at pure 3-banded leather-coloured Italian bees of a good strain. You won't hit the bull's eye every time by a very long way, but you may come near it even when you miss. All over the world honey producers use Italians and it would be foolish to suppose that they do it because these bees have pretty coloured tails. I remember when I was younger and more innocent than I fear I am now, I was much surprised on visiting the apiary of one of our notables who was never tired of holding up for our admiration the great qualities of the English blacks, to find all, or nearly all the hives stocked with Italians, and very yellow ones at that.

(1) - reprinted by Northern Bee Books, 2010
(2) - published by Northern Bee Books, 2011
(s) - republished by Northern Bee Books, 1985

Spring 2012
Convention

Friday 20, Saturday 21, Sunday 22 April

The New Venue

Harper Adams University College Campus, Newport, Shropshire
Set your Sat-Nav for TF10 8NB

For 2012 the BBKA Spring Convention moves to a new venue which offers greatly improved lecture and workshop facilities

Broader programme with new courses and workshops

Bigger and better trade show, all under one roof

Quality, competitively priced accommodation and catering available on site

Easy access via M54 and M6 with good on-site parking

Follow the beekeeping press and the BBKA web-site for more details on the programme
Tickets available in January

General enquiries to Tim Lovett: tjl@dermapharm.co.uk
Trade enquiries to John Hayward: jvhayward@suffolkonline.net

SHERLOCK HOLMES LIVES ON: The Mary Russell/ Sherlock Holmes series, by Laurie R King

Val Phipps

●

Unfinished books or music, completed by others, re-makes of old films, films of books, and new takes on old fictional characters are often regarded with suspicion, and frequently disappoint, even affront. It was, therefore, with interest mixed with trepidation that I approached the first of this series of eleven stories. Liking detective fiction and mystery, and having read the Conan Doyle 'Sherlock Holmes' mysteries in the dim and distant past, I nevertheless retain the impression that the characters are stylised and rigid, and do not develop throughout the series.

I was relieved and surprised to find that central character alive and well, with a new, and female, counterpart, Mary Russell, a fifteen-year-old budding intellectual, both well-rounded characters, the partnership between them developing with sensitivity and wit, but with the basic character of Holmes intact.

These are books for those who like literate, historical, well-researched mystery and suspense novels; not, it must be said, just for beekeepers, despite the first and two subsequent titles; The Beekeeper's Apprentice, The Language of Bees, and The God of the Hive. In these, the beekeeping is incidental, part of his life; Holmes has gone to live in Sussex, ostensibly to spend his retirement studying, amongst other things, bees, but his own volatile character and fate, in the shape of his 'spider in the middle of the web' brother, Mycroft, and a chance meeting with Mary Russell spark off a chain of mysteries which are geographically, politically and culturally wide-ranging.

The American author, Laurie R King, a prolific writer, has produced this series, another very different one, the 'Kate Matinelli' cases, has compiled many anthologies and a list of 'stand alone' novels. Born in 1952, her background is Jewish, and she chose to study comparative religion for her BA, and Old Testament Theology (Feminine Aspects of Yahweh) for her MA. She is a popular lecturer, attending many conferences internationally. Married for many years, until his death in 2009, to the historian Noel Quinton King, she travelled widely and lived in many countries, but was especially fascinated by England, particularly London, the 20's, the Great War and the government and politics of that time, womens' rights and religious expression, all themes woven into the fast-paced and entertaining narratives . Her writing is witty, erudite, and sometimes unmilitantly feminist. She shows her familiarity with other English writers in sly, unexpected ways. For example, she writes Lord Peter Wimsey into a clandestine, incognito cameo appearance; he saves the day and the heroine's bacon with his usual urbane and resouceful style.

Although the actual titles, and the publisher's cover blurbs can sometimes lead to slightly misleading expectations, this is a minor quibble; a very well-educated, well-read, multi-lingual Greek friend has just spent a large part of her summer holiday reading through the complete series, has been totally fascinated by them, feels that they have expanded her knowledge, especially of 'things English', and cannot wait for the novella 'Pirate King', the next in the series, to be published. A telling recommendation!

The Mary Russell / Sherlock Holmes Series:

The Beekeeper's Apprentice (1994)
ISBN: 978-0-312-42736-8

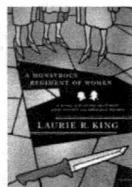

A Monstrous Regiment of Women (1995)
ISBN: 9780312427375

A Letter of Mary (1997)
ISBN: 9780312427382

The Moor (1998)
ISBN: 9780312427399

O Jerusalem (1999)
ISBN: 9780553383249

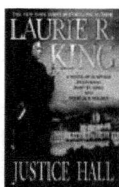

Justice Hall (2002)
ISBN: 9780553381719

The Ga me (2004)
ISBN: 9780553386370

Locked Rooms (2005)
ISBN: 9780553386387

The Language of Bees (2009)
ISBN: 9780553804546

The God of the Hive (2010)
ISBN: 9780553805543

Pirate King (2011)
ISBN: 9780553807981

Beekeeping for Beginners (2011)
E-novella

LAURIE R. KING

THE TARANOV BOARD

John Kinross

People in Straw Houses . . . .

Once again it is time to look at new beekeeping books. Professor Dripitoff, Ina Strainer and myself, the **Taranov Board** (Tomes & reprints and new books - not on varroa), have met at the local cafe, the pub having closed down, to discuss the recently arrived volumes.

On the reprint side it is nice to see A M Foster's **'Bee Boles and Bee Houses'** and Arthur Staniforth's 'Straw and Straw Craftsmen' (both Osprey/ Shire at £4.99 each) back again, although the new idea of putting the pictures above the title makes them impossible to display. All is not yet lost though as the latest title 'Making Craft Cider' by Simon McKie (£7.99) has got the title at the bottom. It has much on Long Ashton Research Station and west country cider with a list of useful items including two tarpaulins and a pot of vaseline. The Professor says this is so if you get very drunk and fall out of a window, your friends can catch you in the two tarpaulins, then your partner can rub the vaseline on the places that are sore.

New books are headed by Thomas Seeley's **'Honeybee Democracy'** (Princeton UP, USA £20.95) which has some wonderful clear pictures both in colour and black and white. Three books just arrived with us here in Hereford are G Lawes' **'The Victorian Beekeeping Revolution'** (Northern Bee Books £16.50) with a foreword by David Charles in which he says "The catalyst of Langstroth's work brought about a transformation in a remarkably short period of time which unfolds within the pages of this book. Most will be amazed as it reveals the extent of time, thought and effort that must have been devoted to all aspects of the craft for its multifold progress during those golden years it covers." The illustrations are of a mixed quality, but note the 'straw storifier' on page 104, which Ina thinks was the place to put her old straws as she always drinks with a straw at home and is still using some she bought wholesale in 1955. Mr Weed's 'foundation machine' looks deadly (page 248) and I especially like the quote on page 224 about attending a

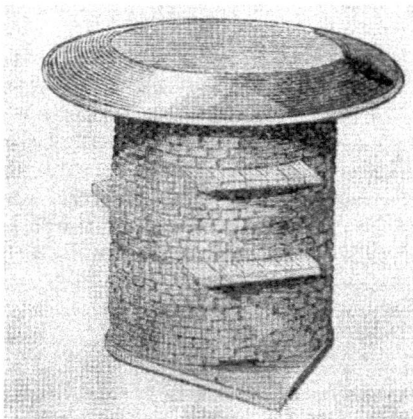

Above: Weed's Foundation Making Machine
Left: Straw Storifier

bee show after a busy week at the office: "For the best part of a week we emerge from our normal quiet into a world of bees, bustle, business, bewitching blue-eyed bar maids and bottled Bass." This is a good book to read through slowly and savour like a good glass of Bass.

'The Bee-friendly Beekeeper' by David Heaf (Northern Bee Books (£24) is for those in favour of top bar hives, like the Warre. The illustrations are excellent, mostly in colour, and there are construction plans. There is much on Nadiring - adding a hive element under an occupied hive, which must be different from an eke, I presume. We have a keen beekeeper in Herefordshire who wanted information on instrumental insemination. The answer is to look at one of the chapters of Eigel Holm's 'Queen Breeding and Genetics' (Northern Bee Books £18) where there is a picture of all the equipment you need in colour. Eigel is a Danish beekeeper but he went to the USA to do a course in insemination. Presumably you need a steady hand for this and the Professor said he couldn't cope ever since he drove his Harley motorbike into a hedge. Ina would like to try but she says she must finish her knitting first.

From Yorkshire comes a useful book for beginners - John Whitaker's **'On the Keeping of Bees'** (£14 from Bee Books New and Old) which has some useful information, a few small colour pictures and much sound advice from an experienced hand.

John Williams, another experienced beekeeper has written **'Starting Out with Bees'** (Bee Craft £15) which lists the tasks from August to July. He covers bee health, queen functions, pros and cons of equipment, etc. John has written on 'Darwins Bees' (Central Association of Beekeepers 2009) as he maintains an observation hive at Darwin's house in Kent where he lives. Like other Bee Craft books there are nice wide margins for notes and sticky finger marks.

Finally, Graham Royle NDB from Cheshire has written his first book: **"Apis through the looking glass'** (Bee Books New and Old £16.99). This is a book of colour photographs of sections of the bee's anatomy based on a lecture Graham gave at Stoneleigh 2009 and again at Aberdeen in 2010.Those students studying anatomy and dissection of honeybees will find it invaluable. It is written to go with IBRA's new edition of Dade's 'Anatomy and Dissection of the Honeybee' (£27.50). For those of you who cannot afford to pay for second-hand copies of the 'Scanning Electronic Atlas of the Honeybee' by Erickson (Second-hand, Bee Books New and Old £235), Graham's book is the answer.

Ina is waiting for the latest joke, which is to do with the weather forecast. It always interrupts the Radio 5 cricket commentary and we turn it on to hear 'Low Faroes' which is not true. The Faroe Islands are certainly not flat. The Professor says it is to do with the tiny entrance door of the Egyptian pyramids and that all Pharoahs, especially his favourite, Ramses the Second, were about five feet high., so next time you hear the weather forecast think of 'Low Pharoahs' and not 'Low Faroes'.

WORD SEARCH

Within this grid there are the names of 32 inventors of beekeeping systems or beekeeping equipment.

The letters can be joined horizontally, vertically or diagonally, either forwards or backwards.

Answers on the next page in the form of anagrams.

```
D Y F Y M X D A D A N T C N S L M R Y P
X B G O K V M U N N N T G A R K I E B M
S N J P H T I M S U O P H M R I Q L L R
X I L S B A T N Z D Z B C F E L R O E L
H U A F R O W J I H R N I F C L E S I F
L Q I E A O M I L L E R V O Y I B Y B J
C I D L U R T O E S I O O H D O U X S H
D G L T F K T J E S Z J P O S N H Q L Y
S M A T Z J U R R E D F O J N Q U W V Q
L M W I W O N H A C X E K P I B R K K G
Z S U L S J E V M Z H V O D M O E L N H
J F F O F E S R E K B O R L M K J I H Y
M K R O U I N O D L I R P G I S R B R E
I U E D Z D E E W Z N G K K S H Q M U L
J N P M I H K S V K G L G U E E I E S L
B Z O W F V C Y S E H E Z M L R P C C A
C B R A N U A M L L A N G S T R O T H Y
A R T R E G M A D Z M S C M Q I O J K M
R Z E R L V P M Z J E N T E R F S X A O
R Y R E V I M K Q A E M Y Y P F C W Y G
```

ANAGRAMS

The answers to the word search are written in the boxes below as anagrams. Rearrange the letters to find the names of the beekeepers.

These words have been mixed up. Can you unscramble them?

MISIMSN	ERK	OLNIIKL	DDANTA	LLYAE	TLTLOOIED
WAERR	EIYLBB	ORHCPPOVOIK	ETRORP	MBNIAHG	NESLGROVE
HAKUCHSR	LRMIEL	ZZIODERN	ALTHTNSORG	ALIADLW	HSMIT
FOAFNHM	REEJNT	EACEMKSNN	OWFR	EDWE	TTUN
FHRSIEFR	BHRUE	AEEDRME	RRAC	YUINQB	NNMU
MHIENRG	ECYD				

OIL SEED RAPE HONEY PRODUCTION

Selby and Willie Robson, father and son commercial bee-farmers from Northumberland, describe the techniques they apply on their 1500 colony bee farm.

From: The Beekeepers Quarterly, No 17, Spring 1989.

Selby and Willie

As in many parts of the British Isles changes in farming practice in North Northumberland have resulted in oilseed rape becoming one of the major sources of blossom honey. As the plant flowers early in the season, good wintering of stocks is essential. We are fortunate here in having access to a number of disused walled gardens which make excellent wintering sites. The hives are placed as close to a south-facing wall as possible. A west-facing wall is also suitable, but not an east-facing wall, as it is important that the sun plays on the hives after mid-day rather than before.

Fresh pollen is necessary for brood rearing so we find that sites with close proximity to villages to be advantageous as there are usually early flowering plants available in the gardens. River banks, too, usually offer a useful selection of plants which give plentiful early pollen.

In beekeeping it is always important to match the number of hives to the available forage at all times of the year. We usually operate hives in lots of 15-20, although 5 or 6 are better. Apiaries of fifty hives or more are out altogether, at least in this part of the world.

Half a dozen colonies on oil seed rape.

By using locations which provide the bees with plentiful forage and shelter the beekeeper can ensure that the morale of his colonies is high, for malnutrition resulting from poorly chosen sites leads inevitably to low morale and disease. Poor handling of colonies and over-inspection of hives can also adversely affect the health of stocks so the beekeeper must always ensure that the

bees are carefully and sensitively manipulated especially during transit and in the early part of the year (our average temperatures are usually about 10 deg. F below those in Southern England).

Our stocks are over-wintered on heather honey. During January we put 4 lbs of fondant wrapped in a polythene bag, with a small tear in it, directly over the cluster and cover this with a potato sack. We are currently developing crownboards with integral insulation and permanent polythene containers to make this type of feeding easier. We find that fondant tends to make the bees begin to breed, although sometimes they ignore it. As stocks use up the fondant we replace it with more.

We never use any type of medication on our bees as the continued use of drugs is likely to cause the bees to lose their natural resistance to parasites.*

At the beginning of the rape flow we like to see colonies with about 4-5 British Standard frames of brood and plenty of young bees. A colony of old bees will require the whole of the rape flow to build up. The ideal is to have colonies that keep pace with the flow and keep egg-laying under control so that a honey crop can be established and retained after the flow is over. This is the result of a long period of acclimatisation to the very unfavourable conditions that prevail in this part of Northumberland. Bees which breed excessively throughout a heavy flow are liable to consume much of the honey if bad weather follows. The message for all beekeepers is "Never buy bees from outside of your area", for the best bees for local conditions will be found in the beekeeper's own apiary. Persevere with them and cull any that are obviously not up to scratch and you will not go far wrong.

Ideally, the hives should be moved onto the rape fields just before the rape begins to flower. Even if the over-wintering site for bees is relatively close to the rape field it is advantageous to get the hives right onto the crop for bees are reluctant to fly any distance at this time of year. Good shelter on the fields is important however, and we always seek out the less windy areas before setting our hives down. Of course all farmers wish to have stocks of bees on their rape crops but some are much more helpful than others. When the hives are being placed on the fields it is advisable to make arrangements with the farmer to have early notification of spraying so that proper precautions can be taken to prevent poisoning of the bees. Again, most farmers are very helpful, either spraying late in the evening or early in the morning and in many cases using sprays which are harmless to bees. If hostathion is used, covering the hives with loose straw in the early morning is very effective in preventing bees from flying, for the straw keeps the hives both cool and dark. There has been very little spraying in this area recently as farmers have found it to be more profitable to seek the advice of the Ministry advisors rather than the representatives of the spray manufacturers before spraying.

Drifting can be a serious problem when bees are moved to new sites early in the year. Young bees which have not had an opportunity to locate the new position of their hive properly, rush out when a nectar flow commences and on returning go into the wrong hive. Soon some hives become overcrowded while others are seriously weakened. The only thing that can be done then is some judicious switching between the weaker and stronger hives or to stand them well apart in the first place, but even this doesn't always work. The worst problem resulting from drifting is that it might lead to swarming from the overcrowded stocks.

With regard to supering, we put on about 1000 supers of drawn comb (the number that we can get off and extract before crystallisation begins) and the subsequent supers are fitted with starter strips of unwired brood foundation about 2.5 cm wide attached with a little hot wax to the top bar of a Manley shallow frame. We use these same supers for producing comb honey for cut-comb flower and heather honey and can be left on the hive or removed as needed. When all the supers are finally removed the rape honey in them can be cut out and warmed to remove crystals before straining. Certainly the unwired supers overcome the granulation problem. Perhaps one day we will get rape honey that doesn't readily granulate.

As far as swarming is concerned we deal with this initially by putting out bait hives rather less than half a mile from each of the rape apiaries. The bait hives are always placed well up from the ground and make use of suitable stands like tree stumps and water troughs. These hives will help to take care of the first swarms because the bees don't fly far afield from the new location in the early part of the year.

After about three weeks at the rape bees that are preparing to swarm may have found the empty hives or holes in trees and more positive precautions have to be taken. We do this by removing supers and tipping the brood box back and looking for queen cells between the combs and then looking down through the combs after removing the excluder. If queen cells are seen a nucleus is made containing a queen cell and the colony and perhaps the adjoining two are removed to a new location about twenty yards away. The nucleus is left in the original site.

Sometimes we make an artificial swarm and leave it on the original site and move away the old brood box. Certainly the colonies which are moved to a new site and lose their flying bees pull down their queen cells, soon get going again, and then make tremendous colonies for the heather.

The tipping method for looking for queen cells is about 90% effective and causes minimal disturbance to the bees.

During 1988 20% of our colonies prepared to swarm and we think we recovered most of them. About 3% became queenless because of the atrocious weather in July which prevented the mating of queens throughout the whole of the month. At one time we reckoned the stocks were holding about 100 lbs each of blossom honey, but this had dropped to 80 lbs by the end of that dreadful month.

Some of the swarming was probably caused by lack of supers as we just could not get to the long distance apiaries quickly enough during the good weather in June.

I am in complete agreement with Mr Wallace of the Quince Honey Farm, Devon, when he said at a lecture he gave in Glasgow that he thought the only way to make a living from bees nowadays was to keep more colonies than one could look after properly. Then, when a good season comes along, all the stocks would get a lot of honey and probably enough to see the bee farmer through one or two bad seasons.

* Written well before varroa reached Northumberland. Editor.

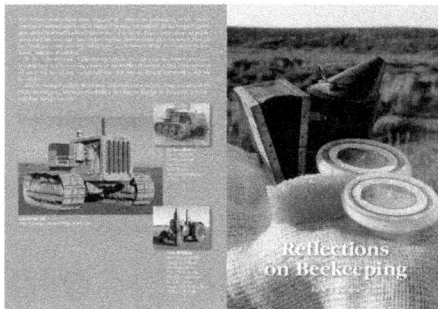

An up-to-date account of Willie Robson's experiences and thoughts on beekeeping matters - *'Reflections on Beekeeping'* was published in the autumn by Northern Bee Books.

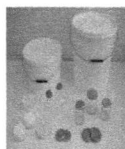

DIARY & CALENDAR

- PART II -

*SR (SUNRISE) SS (SUNSET) FOR LONDON UK.

CALENDAR AND DIARY
With weather lore from *'Weather Lore'*
by Richard Inwards, Rider and Company, 1950.

JANUARY

If a cat licks itself with its face facing the north,
the wind will change to that cold quarter.

Leave the bees alone apart from hefting hives to see if the bees have stores. If light feed candy. This is best done by placing a candy board over the whole of the top of the frames; this will help prevent isolation starvation should there be a very prolonged cold spell. Bees in hives covered in snow will come to no harm - but the light reflecting off the snow may draw bees out to a chilly death. Place boards against the hives to reduce the light entering the hives.

DAY	JANUARY 2012 FORAGE	TEMP		WIND		CL'D	RAIN	1	2	3
		MIN	MAX	DIR	B.S				HIVE WEIGHT	
1										
2										
3										
4										
5										
6										
7										
8										
9										
10										
11										
12										
13										
14										
15										
16										
17										
18										
19										
20										
21										
22										
23										
24										
25										
26										
27										
28										
29										
30										
31										

JAN12

	8,SU SR 08:04, SS 16:10
1,SU NEW YEAR'S DAY	**9,MO** ○
2,MO BANK HOLIDAY	**10,TU**
3,TU	**11,WE**
4,WE	**12,TH**
5,TH	**13,FR**
6,FR	14,SA
7,SA	**15,SU** SR 08:00, SS 16:20

16,MO	**24,TU**
17,TU	**25,WE**
18,WE	**26,TH**
19,TH	**27,FR**
20,FR	28,SA
21,SA	29,SU SR 07:44, SS 16:43
22,SU SR 07:53, SS 16:31	**30,MO**
23,MO ●	**31,TU**

FEBRUARY

Three hoar (or white) frosts are followed by rain.

Forage plants begin to flower, most of them offering plentiful pollen which will help to build up the colony. In areas short of pollen, pollen substitutes or supplements can be given - either on the hive or in specially made outdoor feeders. Useful recipes include:

1. Pollen Patty Substitute: Dissolve 3.5 lb of sugar in 16 oz of boiling water; stir in 1 lb soya flour ensuring that there is a thorough mix. While still hot spread in quarter inch thick pieces on waxed paper measuring about 10 inches square. Turn the patty onto the top of the frames so it is in direct contact with the cluster.

2. Pollen Supplement: 3 - 4 lb of pollen (from own bees or a reputable source) is mixed with 21 lb sugar, to this mixture water to ten times of the volume is added and then kneaded into a stiff dough. Soak overnight in water and then add to the top of the brood nest. Ken Stevens advises that no pollen supplement/substitute should be supplied in a dry state - as in the photo here - but I did see bees collecting pollen substitutes in this form in an outdoor feeder at Craibstone, Aberdeen, at the time of Bernard Mobus.

DAY	FEBRUARY 2012 FORAGE	TEMP		WIND		CL'D	RAIN	1	2	3
		MIN	MAX	DIR	B.S			HIVE WEIGHT		
1										
2										
3										
4										
5										
6										
7										
8										
9										
10										
11										
12										
13										
14										
15										
16										
17										
18										
19										
20										
21										
22										
23										
24										
25										
26										
27										
28										

FEB12

	8,WE
1,WE	**9,TH**
2,TH CANDLEMAS DAY	**10,FR**
3,FR	11,SA
4,SA	12,SU SR 07:21, SS 17:09
5,SU SR 07:33, SS 16:56	13,MO
6,MO	**14,TU** ST VALENTINE'S DAY
7,TU ●	**15,WE**

16,TH	**24,FR**
17,FR	25,SA
18,SA	26,SU SR 06:53, SS 17:34
19,SU SR 07:08, SS 17:22	**27,MO**
20,MO	**28,TU**
21,TU ○	**29,WE**
22,WE	
23,TH	

MARCH

Magpies flying three or four together and
uttering harsh cries predict windy weather.

Bees will be flying more frequently, but winter is not over. Many bees die at this time of year from starvation. Check food stores frequently and feed if necessary. Check out-apiaries for storm damage. Bees are tough - they can survive in upturned hives even with exposed combs for a short period of time, but the longer they are left in this condition the more vulnerable they will be to predators as well as to the increasing effects of the weather.

DAY	MARCH 2012 FORAGE	TEMP		WIND		CL'D	RAIN	1	2	3
		MIN	MAX	DIR	B.S			HIVE WEIGHT		
1										
2										
3										
4										
5										
6										
7										
8										
9										
10										
11										
12										
13										
14										
15										
16										
17										
18										
19										
20										
21										
22										
23										
24										
25										
26										
27										
28										
29										
30										
31										

MAR12

	8,TH
1,TH	**9,FR**
2,FR	10,SA
3,SA	11,SU SR 06:23, SS 17:59
4,SU SR 06:38, SS 17:47	**12,MO** ●
5,MO	**13,TU**
6,TU	**14,WE**
7,WE	**15,TH**

16,FR	24,SA
17,SA BANK HOLIDAY ST PATRICK'S DAY NORTHERN IRELAND	25,SU SR 06:51, SS 19:23
18,SU SR 06:07, SS 18:11	**26,MO**
19,MO	**27,TU** ●
20,TU	**28,WE**
21,WE	**29,TH**
22,TH	**30,FR**
23,FR	31,SA

APRIL

If it thunders on All Fools' Day,
it brings good crops of corn and hay.

Spring should be here now, but cold winds can be a problem, particularly in the east. First examinations, as brief as possible, should be made to ensure that the colony is queen right and healthy and also has good reserves of food and storage space for incoming nectar.

DAY	APRIL 2012 FORAGE	TEMP MIN	MAX	WIND DIR	B.S	CL'D	RAIN	1	2	3 HIVE WEIGHT
1										
2										
3										
4										
5										
6										
7										
8										
9										
10										
11										
12										
13										
14										
15										
16										
17										
18										
19										
20										
21										
22										
23										
24										
25										
26										
27										
28										
29										
30										

APR12

	8,SU SR 06:19, SS 19:46
1,SU SR 06:35, SS 19:34	**9,MO** BANK HOLIDAY EASTER MONDAY
2,MO	**10,TU**
3,TU	**11,WE**
4,WE	**12,TH**
5,TH	**13,FR**
6,FR ● BANK HOLIDAY GOOD FRIDAY	**14,SA**
7,SA	**15,SU** * SR 06:04, SS 19:58

16,MO	**24,TU**
17,TU	**25,WE**
18,WE	**26,TH**
19,TH	**27,FR**
20,FR **	28,SA
21,SA ○ **	29,SU SR 05:36, SS 20:21
22,SU ** SR 05:49, SS 20:09	**30,MO**
23,MO	* ORTHODOX EASTER ** BBKA SPRING CONVENTION, HARPER ADAMS UNIVERSITY COLLEGE CAMPUS, NEWPORT, SHROPSHIRE TF10 8NB

MAY

Swarming time is nigh, so be prepared. Have all the things you need ready on hand to capture a swarm; a skep (or suitable box), secateurs, small saw, a piece of cloth. You should have already worked out your strategy for swarm control and have nuc boxes awaiting splits if you intend to increase your stocks. Despite the best laid plans the weather can interrupt your schedule, the result being that when you open the hive you are met by the squawking sound of imprisoned queens or queens emerging from their cells and running quickly over the combs or even attempting to fly around. Bait hives should be set up now, at least 2 - 3 metres above the ground, with some old comb to attract the house hunting bees.

DAY	MAY 2012 FORAGE	TEMP MIN	MAX	WIND DIR	B.S	CL'D	RAIN	1	2	3 HIVE WEIGHT
1										
2										
3										
4										
5										
6										
7										
8										
9										
10										
11										
12										
13										
14										
15										
16										
17										
18										
19										
20										
21										
22										
23										
24										
25										
26										
27										
28										
29										
30										
31										

MAY12

	8,TU
1,TU	**9,WE**
2,WE	**10,TH**
3,TH	**11,FR**
4,FR	12,SA
5,SA	13,SU SR 05:11, SS 20:43
6,SU ● SR 05:23, SS 20:32	**14,MO**
7,MO EARLY MAY BANK HOLIDAY	**15,TU**

16,WE	**24,TH**
17,TH	**25,FR**
18,FR	26,SA
19,SA	27,SU SR 04:53, SS 21:03
20,SU ○ SR 05:01, SS 20:54	**28,MO** SPRING BANK HOLIDAY
21,MO	**29, TU**
22,TU	**30, WE**
23,WE	**31, TH**

JUNE

When the bramble blossoms in early June,
an early harvest is expected.

The bees should be happy foraging now, taking the last of the oil seed rape and early flowering trees. Keep the frames clean by removing brace and burr comb and replace three old brood combs from each hive with new frames fitted with foundation. The pieces of collected comb and the old comb cut out from the frames should be placed in a wax extractor now that the sun is beginning to warm things up.

DAY	JUNE 2012 FORAGE	TEMP		WIND		CL'D	RAIN	1	2	3
		MIN	MAX	DIR	B.S			HIVE WEIGHT		
1										
2										
3										
4										
5										
6										
7										
8										
9										
10										
11										
12										
13										
14										
15										
16										
17										
18										
19										
20										
21										
22										
23										
24										
25										
26										
27										
28										
29										
30										

JUN12

	8,FR
1,FR	9,SA
2,SA	10,SU SR 04:44, SS 21:17
3,SU SR 04:47, SS 21:11	**11,MO**
4,MO ● BANK HOLIDAY QUEEN'S DIAMOND JUBILEE	**12,TU**
5,TU	**13,WE**
6,WE	**14,TH**
7,TH	**15,FR**

16,SA	24,SU * SR 04:44, SS 21:22
17,SU SR 04:43, SS 21:20	25,MO
18,MO	26,TU
19,TU ○	27,WE
20,WE	28,TH
21,TH SUMMER SOLSTICE	29,FR
22,FR	30,SA
23,SA	

JULY

When black snails on the road you see.
Then on the morrow rain will be.

Most of the summer honey will be extracted by now although in some districts the limes, blackberry and willow herb will give further forage. Whilst extracting, look carefully at the way in which the bees have capped the honey. Ideally there should be a slight gap between the honey and the capping. This makes it easier for the wax to be removed with an uncapping knife. However, nature's purpose was this;. the more convex cappings allow for expansion of honey within the comb thus preventing weeping of honey which could lead to fermentation within the hive during the winter months. Bees which have good cappings are worth propagating, not only for the general health of the colony, but also because they are good for producing section or cut comb honey.

DAY	JULY 2012 FORAGE	TEMP		WIND		CL'D	RAIN	1	2	3
		MIN	MAX	DIR	B.S			HIVE WEIGHT		
1										
2										
3										
4										
5										
6										
7										
8										
9										
10										
11										
12										
13										
14										
15										
16										
17										
18										
19										
20										
21										
22										
23										
24										
25										
26										
27										
28										
29										
30										
31										

JUL12

	8,SU SR 04:54, SS 21:17
1,SU SR 04:48, SS 21:21	9,MO
2,MO EARLY MAY BANK HOLIDAY	10,TU
3,TU ●	11,WE
4,WE	12,TH
5,TH	13,FR
6,FR	14,SA
7,SA	15,SU SR 05:01, SS 21:11

16,MO	**24,TU** FIBKA - GORMANSTON CONVENTION
17,TU	**25,WE** FIBKA - GORMANSTON CONVENTION
18,WE	**26,TH** FIBKA - GORMANSTON CONVENTION
19,TH ○	**27,FR** FIBKA - GORMANSTON CONVENTION
20,FR	28,SA
21,SA	29,SU SR 05:20, SS 20:53
22,SU SR 05:10, SS 21:03 FIBKA - GORMANSTON CONVENTION	**30,MO**
23,MO FIBKA - GORMANSTON CONVENTION	**31,TU**

AUGUST

*A singing in the ear sometimes indicates a change in the weather
due to a rise in pressure.*

Honey extraction will continue followed by feeding and the first of the late summer varroa treatments. About 100g of icing sugar should be sprinkled over the top bars of each hive and brushed over the seams of bees. Three or four applications, each a week apart, provides the beekeeper with a cheap, effective and organic method of varroa control. Should a backup be necessary, two applications of Apiguard, two weeks apart, should keep the bees relatively free of varroa for many months ahead. Those beekeepers taking their hives to the heather moors have the possibility of having a crop of excellent, well sought after honey which always commands a good price. Furthermore, heather honey left in the combs for bees to overwinter on will get bees off to a flying start in spring because of the high proportion of pollen the honey contains.

DAY	AUGUST 2012 FORAGE	TEMP MIN	TEMP MAX	WIND DIR	WIND B.S	CL'D	RAIN	1	2	3
								HIVE WEIGHT		
1										
2										
3										
4										
5										
6										
7										
8										
9										
10										
11										
12										
13										
14										
15										
16										
17										
18										
19										
20										
21										
22										
23										
24										
25										
26										
27										
28										
29										
30										
31										

AUG12

	8,WE
1,WE	**9,TH**
2,TH ●	**10,FR**
3,FR	11,SA
4,SA	12,SU SR 05:42, SS 20:28 FIRST DAY OF GROUSE SHOOTING - TRADITIONAL TIME FOR TAKING BEES TO THE HEATHER MOORS.
5,SU SR 05:31, SS 20:41	**13,MO**
6,MO	**14,TU**
7,TU	**15,WE**

16,TH	**24,FR** ST BARTHOLOMEW'S DAY, TRADITIONAL DAY FOR HARVESTING HONEY
17,FR ○	25,SA
18,SA	26,SU SR 06:04, SS 19:59
19,SU SR 05:53, SS 20:14	**27,MO** SUMMER BANK HOLIDAY
20,MO	28,TU
21,TU	29,WE
22,WE	30,TH
23,TH	**31,FR** ● (BLUEMOON)

SEPTEMBER

The moon in a halo indicates a storm and the
number of stars contained the number of days of stormy weather.

Bees will be brought back from the moors and winter feeding should begin - not just to build up the food reserves but to keep the queen laying so that there will be plentiful young 'winter' bees on whose work the hive depends in early spring. Bees will continue to look for suitable forage so beekeepers are encouraged to grow early autumn flowering plants such as Michaelmas Daisies, Golden Rod, Buddleias, Sunflowers, Hollyhocks etc - all of which should provide nectar and pollen until the first frosts. Without suitable flowers bees might turn to fallen fruit and compete with the wasps, hornets and other insects who are also on the lookout for sources of carbohydrate. Hives will be increasingly bothered by wasps and hornets now, so suitable trapping methods should be devised.

DAY	SEPTEMBER 2012 FORAGE	TEMP MIN	TEMP MAX	WIND DIR	WIND B.S	CL'D	RAIN	1	2	3 HIVE WEIGHT
1										
2										
3										
4										
5										
6										
7										
8										
9										
10										
11										
12										
13										
14										
15										
16										
17										
18										
19										
20										
21										
22										
23										
24										
25										
26										
27										
28										
29										
30										

SEP12

	8,SA
1,SA	9,SU SR 06:26, SS 19:28
2,SU SR 06:15, SS 19:44	10,MO
3,MO	11,TU
4,TU	12,WE
5,WE	13,TH
6,TH	14,FR
7,FR	15,SA

16,SU ○ SR 06:37, SS 19:12	24,MO
17,MO	25,TU
18,TU	26,WE
19,WE	27,TH
20,TH	28,FR
21,FR	29,SA
22,SA	30,SU ● SR 07:00, SS 18:40
23,SU SR 06:49, SS 18:56 AUTUMN EQUINOX	

OCTOBER

*When squirrels lay in a store of nuts expect a hard winter;
if they eat the nuts on the tree the winter will be mild.*

Winter feeding should be completed by now. With the last feeds add thymol to the syrup to help prevent nosema disease which is becoming a serious problem, especially as *Nosema cerana* has become widespread (20g Thymol dissolved in 100 ml of alcohol/ surgical spirit - 1 ml added to each 3 litres of sugar syrup). Ivy will continue to give work for the bees on mild days and under certain conditions a good flow could provide a beekeeper with an extra box of honey. Mouseguards should be put on the hive entrances and in areas where woodpeckers abound, a cylinder of wire netting should be placed around each hive. For good measure put a brick on each roof to keep it in place during the wilder and stormy days of autumn and winter.

DAY	OCTOBER 2012 FORAGE	TEMP		WIND		CL'D	RAIN	1	2	3
		MIN	MAX	DIR	B.S			HIVE WEIGHT		
1										
2										
3										
4										
5										
6										
7										
8										
9										
10										
11										
12										
13										
14										
15										
16										
17										
18										
19										
20										
21										
22										
23										
24										
25										
26										
27										
28										
29										
30										
31										

OCT12

	8,MO
1,MO	**9,TU**
2,TU	**10,WE**
3,WE	**11,TH**
4,TH	**12,FR**
5,FR	13,SA ○
6,SA	14,SU SR 07:23, SS 18:09
7,SU SR 07:12, SS 18:24	**15,MO** ○

16,TU	**24,WE**
17,WE	**25,TH** NATIONAL HONEY SHOW
18,TH	**26,FR** NATIONAL HONEY SHOW
19,FR	27,SA NATIONAL HONEY SHOW
20,SA	28,SU SR 06:48, SS 16:40 CLOCKS GO BACK ONE HOUR
21,SU SR 07:35, SS 17:54	**29,MO** ●
22,MO	**30,TU**
23,TU	**31,WE**

NOVEMBER

*When the field mouse makes its burrow with the opening to the south,
it expects a severe winter; when to the north it expects much rain.*

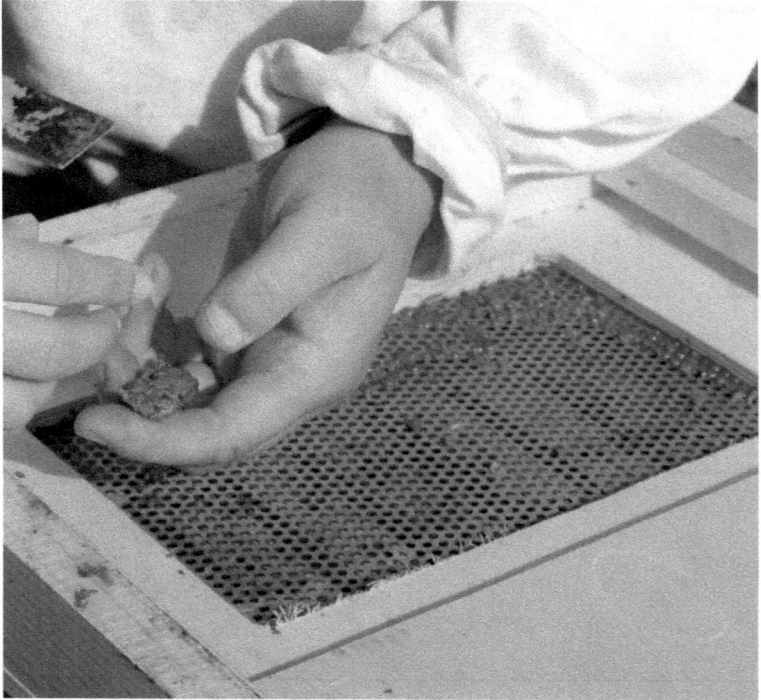

All hives should be given a last check for the winter to ensure that they are weatherproof, stable on their stands with the floors slightly sloping down to the front to prevent water from entering the hive. Extracted combs should be stored in a mouse and rat proof place having previously been sprayed with B401 to prevent damage by waxmoths, With the colder weather it should be easier to scrape propolis away from hive parts or propolis screens. The propolis can then be cleaned and dissolved in alcohol to make many useful medicinal products.

DAY	NOVEMBER 2012 FORAGE	TEMP		WIND		CL'D	RAIN	1	2	3
		MIN	MAX	DIR	B.S			HIVE WEIGHT		
1										
2										
3										
4										
5										
6										
7										
8										
9										
10										
11										
12										
13										
14										
15										
16										
17										
18										
19										
20										
21										
22										
23										
24										
25										
26										
27										
28										
29										
30										

NOV12

	8,TH
1,TH	**9,FR**
2,FR	10,SA
3,SA	11,SU SR 07:12, SS 16:16
4,SU SR 07:00, SS 16:28	**12,MO**
5,MO	**13,TU** ○
6,TU	**14,WE**
7,WE	**15,TH**

16,FR	24,SA
17,SA	25,SU SR 07:35, SS 15:59
18,SU SR 07:24, SS 16:07	**26,MO**
19,MO	**27,TU**
20,TU	**28,WE** ●
21,WE	**29,TH**
22,TH	**30,FR**
23,FR	

DECEMBER

Hares take to the open country before a snowstorm.

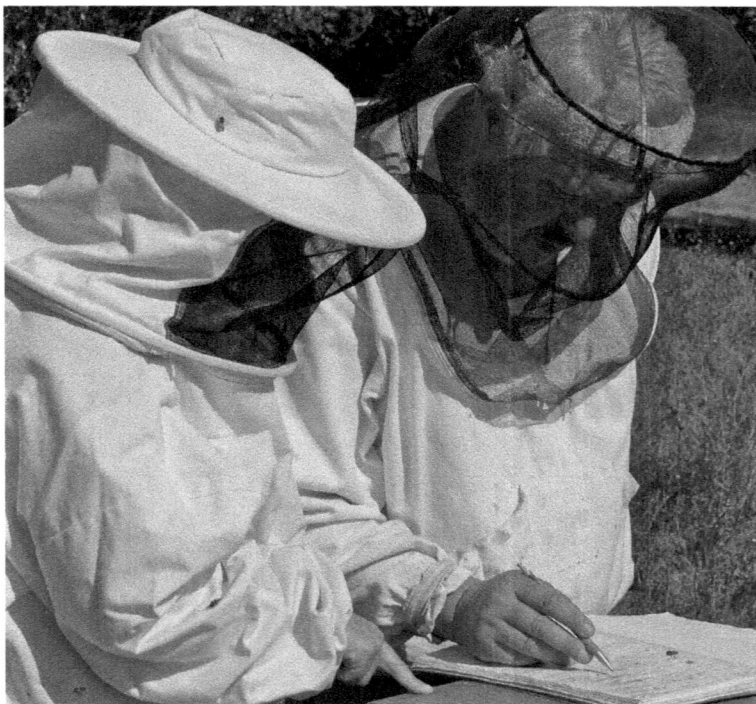

December was always a quiet time in the apiary with nothing for the beekeeper to do except to check that the hives were still in place on their stands and that mouse guards hadn't fallen away. Now though, more and more beekeepers are using this seemingly broodless time in the colony's cycle to apply oxalic acid as an organic method of varroa control. With the changing climate it is my guess that a proportion of brood could still be present in the hive and together with the fact that the bees have to be disturbed (be it only briefly), I would prefer other efficient non-chemical methods of varroa control. I was always under the impression that a hive disturbed unnecessarily could lead to the loss of the queen; it would be interesting to see if this is one of the reasons why stocks become queenless in spring. So, December; another year gone by. Hopefully, candles and honey to sell at Christmas fairs or to give as presents, plenty of books to read on beekeeping in front of a roaring fire and, as the New Year approaches, going through the notes made in the apiaries so that plans can be made for the forthcoming season.

DAY	DECEMBER 2012 FORAGE	TEMP		WIND		CL'D	RAIN	1	2	3
		MIN	MAX	DIR	B.S			HIVE WEIGHT		
1										
2										
3										
4										
5										
6										
7										
8										
9										
10										
11										
12										
13										
14										
15										
16										
17										
18										
19										
20										
21										
22										
23										
24										
25										
26										
27										
28										
29										
30										
31										

DEC12

	8,SA
1,SA	**9,SU** SR 07:54, SS 15:52
2,SU SR 07:46, SS 15:54	**10,MO**
3,MO	**11,TU**
4,TU	**12,WE**
5,WE	**13,TH** ○
6,TH	**14,FR**
7,FR ST AMBROSE DAY - PATRON SAINT OF BEEKEEPERS	**15,SA**

16,SU SR 08:01, SS 15:52	**24,MO**
17,MO	**25,TU** CHRISTMAS DAY BANK HOLIDAY
18,TU	**26,WE** BOXING DAY BANK HOLIDAY
19,WE	**27,TH**
20,TH	**28,FR** ●
21,FR WINTER SOLSTICE	29,SA
22,SA	30,SU SR 08:06, SS 16:00
23,SU SR 08:05, SS 15:55	**31,MO**

Hive/ Q NO.	Year Q Raised	Frames of Brood Autumn 2011	Combs Covered	Honey Stored- Sugar fed Kg	Combs Covered Spring 2012	Frames of Brood Spring 2012	Spring Feeding Kg	Queens Reared	Nuclei
1									
2									
3									
4									
5									
6									
7									
8									
9									
10									
11									
12									
13									
14									
15									
16									
17									
18									
19									
20									
21									
22									
23									
24									

HONEYBEE COLONIES

1									
2									
3									
4									
5									
6									
7									
8									
9									
10									
11									
12									
13									
14									
15									
16									
17									
18									
19									
20									
21									
22									
23									
24									

BEEEKEEPING RECORDS

Number	items	Est. Value	
		£	P
	Stocks of Bees		
	Empty Hives		
	Combs - Deep - Shallow		
	Frames		
	Foundations		
	Honey Extractor		
	Honey Tanks		
	Other items		
	Honey Jars		
	Honey		

JANUARY 2013

S	M	T	W	T	F	S
		1	2	3	4	5
6	7	8	9	10	11	12
13	14	15	16	17	18	19
20	21	22	23	24	25	26
27	28	29	30	31		

FEBRUARY 2013

S	M	T	W	T	F	S
					1	2
3	4	5	6	7	8	9
10	11	12	13	14	15	16
17	18	19	20	21	22	23
24	25	26	27	28		

MARCH 2013

S	M	T	W	T	F	S
					1	2
3	4	5	6	7	8	9
10	11	12	13	14	15	16
17	18	19	20	21	22	23
24	25	26	27	28	29	30
31						

APRIL 2013

S	M	T	W	T	F	S
	1	2	3	4	5	6
7	8	9	10	11	12	13
14	15	16	17	18	19	20
21	22	23	24	25	26	27
28	29	30				

MAY 2013

S	M	T	W	T	F	S
			1	2	3	4
5	6	7	8	9	10	11
12	13	14	15	16	17	18
19	20	21	22	23	24	25
26	27	28	29	30	31	

JUNE 2013

S	M	T	W	T	F	S
						1
2	3	4	5	6	7	8
9	10	11	12	13	14	15
16	17	18	19	20	21	22
23	24	25	26	27	28	29
30						

JULY 2013

S	M	T	W	T	F	S
	1	2	3	4	5	6
7	8	9	10	11	12	13
14	15	16	17	18	19	20
21	22	23	24	25	26	27
28	29	30	31			

AUGUST 2013

S	M	T	W	T	F	S
				1	2	3
4	5	6	7	8	9	10
11	12	13	14	15	16	17
18	19	20	21	22	23	24
25	26	27	28	29	30	31

SEPTEMBER 2013

S	M	T	W	T	F	S
1	2	3	4	5	6	7
8	9	10	11	12	13	14
15	16	17	18	19	20	21
22	23	24	25	26	27	28
29	30					

OCTOBER 2013

S	M	T	W	T	F	S
		1	2	3	4	5
6	7	8	9	10	11	12
13	14	15	16	17	18	19
20	21	22	23	24	25	26
27	28	29	30	31		

NOVEMBER 2013

S	M	T	W	T	F	S
					1	2
3	4	5	6	7	8	9
10	11	12	13	14	15	16
17	18	19	20	21	22	23
24	25	26	27	28	29	30

DECEMBER 2013

S	M	T	W	T	F	S
1	2	3	4	5	6	7
8	9	10	11	12	13	14
15	16	17	18	19	20	21
22	23	24	25	26	27	28
29	30	31				

All efforts have been made to ensure the accuracy of the information in these pages. Corrections and amendments should be sent to The Editor The Beekeepers Annual, c/o Northern Bee Books, Scout Bottom Farm, Mytholmroyd, Hebden Bridge HX7 5JS

DIRECTORY, ASSOCIATIONS AND SERVICES

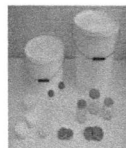

DIRECTORY, ASSOCIATIONS AND SERVICES

BEE MAILING

✉ ☎

BEEKEEPING MAILING LISTS

http://www.zbee.dircon.co.uk

Beekeeping mailing list services provided by zbee.com http://www.zbee. dircon.co.uk

KENT BEEKEEPERS ASSOCIATION, THE

Name of mailing list: Kentbee-L Serving a possible membership of 400. **Support website:** http://www.kentbee.com Approximately 80 have subscribed. Providing a forum for local branch announcements and news and chat about beekeeping. **To subscribe to Kentbee-L send a message to:** mailserver@zbee.com **Subject field:** You leave this blank it doesn't matter. **In the message body write:** Subscribe Kentbee-L then send the message and await further instructions to complete the subscription process.

NATIONAL HONEY SHOW, THE

Name of mailing list: NHS The National Honey Show is held in October each year in London, the support website http://www.honeyshow.co.uk has more information and schedules, **To subscribe to NHS send a message to:** mailserver@zbee.com, **Subject field:** You leave this blank it doesn't matter., **In the message body write:** Subscribe NHS then send the message and await further instructions to complete the subscription process

BEE IMPROVEMENT & BEE BREEDERS ASSOCIATION, THE (BIBBA)

Name of mailing list: BIBBA-L, Support website http://www.bibba.com/, **To subscribe to BIBBA-L send a message to:** mailserver@zbee.com, **Subject field:** You leave this blank it doesn't matter. **In the message body write:** Subscribe BIBBA-L then send the message and await further instructions to complete the subscription process.

✉ ☎

APINET (BEEKEEPING EDUCATION EXTENSION NETWORK)
Name of mailing list: APINETL, Support website n/a, **To subscribe send a message to:** mailserver@zbee.com, **Subject field:** You leave this blank it doesn't matter.
In the message body write: Subscribe APINETL then send the message and await further instructions to complete the subscription process.

BROMLEY & SIDCUP & ORPINGTON BEEKEEPERS ASSOCIATION
Name of mailing list: BBK, **Support website:** http://www. kentbee.com/, **To subscribe to BBK send a message to:** mailserver@zbee.com, **Subject field:** You leave this blank it doesn't matter. **In the message body write:** Subscribe BBK then send the message and await further instructions to complete the subscription process.

THE BRITISH BEEKEEPERS ASOCIATION (BBKA)
Name of mailing list: BBKA, **Support website:** http://www. bbka.org.uk, Private list members only, see members area for joining details.

BDI

BEE DISEASES INSURANCE LTD

SECRETARY
Donald Robertson-Adams
Bryngwrog
Beulah, Newcastle Emlyn
Ceredigion, SA38 9QR
07532 336076
donald@theoldmill.fsnet.
co.uk

TREASURER AND
SCHEME B MANAGER
Mrs Sharon Blake
Stratton Court,
South Petherton,
Somerset TA13 5LQ
01460 242124
sbeditor@yahoo.co.uk

CLAIMS MANAGER
Bernard Diaper
57 Marfield Close,
Walmley,
Sutton Coldfield B76 1YD
0121 3133112
b.diaper@tiscali.co.uk

PRESIDENT
Richard Ball
Stoneyford Farmhouse
Colaton Raleigh
Sidmouth
Devon, EX10 0HZ
01395 567990
richard.ball@fera.gsi.
gov.uk

Bee Diseases Insurance (BDI) provides insurance cover for individual beekeepers, association apiaries and commercial beekeepers alike, against the possibility of their bees and equipment being destroyed as a result of a Destruction Order following a visit from an authorised Bee Inspector. .

BDI provides compensation for specified property that may need to be destroyed as a result of American Foul Brood and European Foul Brood.

BDI has established a contingency fund capped at £25,000 a year if Small Hive Beetle or Tropilaelaps infestation is found.

Scheme A provides cover for the beekeeper with a total of 39 colonies or less. Cover is obtained by being a member of a Beekeeping Association that is a member of BDI Ltd.

Scheme B provides cover for beekeepers with 40 or more colonies in total. Insurance under this Scheme is on a personal basis and further details can be obtained from the Scheme B Manager.

REMEMBER: DISEASE CAN STRIKE ANY COLONY AT ANY TIME AND IT IS SPREAD THROUGHOUT THE COUNTRY. PROTECT YOUR APIARY, AND OTHER BEEKEEPERS, THROUGH B.D.I.

BEE FARMERS' ASSOCIATION OF THE UNITED KINGDOM

BEE FARMERS' ASSOCIATION

The BFA represents the professional beekeepers of the UK.

The association is the largest contract pollinator in the UK and our members are responsible for virtually all the migratory pollination. They are expected to have a good degree of competence; membership requires over 40 hives, and sponsorship by a BFA member who knows the applicant as a beekeeper. We have recently introduced a code of conduct which members are expected to observe. In addition we have a significant number of members who get some income from being bee inspectors, responsible for identifying and dealing with notifiable disease.

We have one business meeting a year which follows the Annual General Meeting in April at Stoneleigh on the same Saturday as the BBKA convention. Business is also conducted at twice-yearly regional meetings which pass items up to the main meeting for discussion and voting, and which put forward candidates for the committee.

The BFA is affiliated to the National Farmers Union and The Honey (Packers) Association with whom we work effectively in promoting ecological sensitive farming and in promoting consumer awareness through events such 'National Honey Week' and bulk sales to retail chains.

MEMBERSHIP

Our members are expected to have a good degree of competence.

FULL MEMBERSHIP requires over 40 hives, and sponsorship by a BFA member who knows the applicant as a beekeeper.

ASSOCIATE MEMBERSHIP is a stepping stone to full membership of the BFA for beekeepers with a minimum of 20 hives and who would like to take up commercial or semi-commercial beekeeping.

Membership forms are available from the Membership Secretary, or as a download from our website.

FUNCTIONS

- To monitor and to keep members informed about developments in commercial beekeeping, bee science

CHAIRMAN, John Home
Northcote
Deppers Bridge
Southam,
Warwickshire
CV47 2SU
01926 612 322
northcote4home@
btinternet.com

VICE CHAIRMAN,
Robin Lewis
4 Meadow View,
Llanfihangel,
Talyllyn,
Brecon.
LD3 7TX
01874 658466

TREASURER,
Mr. D. Isles
Hudnalls Apiary
The Hudnalls, St Briavels
Lydney Gloucestershire
GL15 5RT
dougisles@yahoo.co.uk

SECRETARY, J. Howat
8 Olivers Close
West Totton
Southampton SO40 8FH
02380 907850
02380 907850
john@eclipse01.
demon.co.uk

BFA

✉ ☎

POLLINATION SEC,
Alan Hart
61 Fakenham Road,
Great Witchingham,
Norwich,
NORFOLK
NR9 5AE
01603 308911
earlswoodbees@hotmail.
co.uk

BULLETIN EDITOR,
David Bancalari
Park Farm Barn
Shortthorn Road
Stratton Strawless
Norfolk
NR10 5NX
David@
Bancalari.fslife.co.uk

MEMBERSHIP SECRETARY
Gerry Fry
2, The Glade,
Waterlooville
Hants
PO7 7PD
02392 520075
gerry_fry@sky.com

and UK and EEC legislation.
- Liaison with Farmers, Growers, Contractors, Consumers and other organisations.
- Liaison with UK Government Departments dealing with beekeeping, medicines, and allied matters.
- Liaison and co-operation with UK Beekeeping organisations.
- Contact with European beekeeping organisations (EPBA) and representation on the EEC Honey Working Party (COPA/COGECA) in Brussels.
- Political lobbying through MPs and Euro MPs.
- Member of the Confederation of National Beekeeping Associations (CONBA)
- Member of the European Professional Beekeepers' Association (EPBA)
- Associate member of the Honey Association

FACILITIES FOR MEMBERS:
- Bi-monthly Bulletins with news and updates, notes on meetings with DEFRA, Fera, VMD, and the EEC, reports on current beekeeping problems (e.g. varroa) and commercial developments world-wide.. This bulletin is available as a paper and/or an e-document
  * e-news. Frequent electronic updates on news items
- Free advertisement of members' sales and wants (including hive products, bee stocks and spare equipment).
* Regional meetings which provide for local discussion and opportunities for trading between members.
- Crop and winter loss reports.
- Free Circulation among members of UK and foreign magazines.
- Free insurance for products and third party liability (not limited to thirty hives).
- Special rates for employers liability insurance.
- Comprehensive special beefarmers insurance with the NFU.
- Pollination contracts.
- Advice from experienced members on all aspects of honey farming and commercial beekeeping; sources of equipment and sundries.
- Product directory listing specialist suppliers.
- Discounts from suppliers.
- Bulk purchase schemes to minimize costs to individual members..

ANNUAL CONVENTION WEEKEND
- Spring meeting for members and partners, held each March at different locations in the UK or abroad. Visits to local bee and research establishments; lectures and discussions on bee-related matters; sight seeing, and social events.

BEEKEEPING COURSES & SERVICES

PART TIME LECTURERS & FURTHER EDUCATION COURSES IN BEEKEEPING

The following may offer a range of theoretical and practical courses in beekeeping, in some cases an advisory service or a diagnostic service for adult bee diseases only may be offered.

The range of services and activities is wide and this list is not exhaustive but the following may be contacted for details of facilities in an enquirer's area.

BEDFORDSHIRE,
Mike Nieman
43 Flitwick Road
Westoning
Bedfordshire
MK45 5JA
01525 717040
Harry Inman
10 Constable Hill
Bedford
MK41 7LJ
01234 306554
* Beekeeping for Beginners
* Practical Beekeeping

BERKSHIRE COLLEGE OF AGRICULTURE, Kate Malenczuk and Reg Hook
Hall Place,
Burchetts Green
Maidenhead,
Berkshire SL6 6QR
www.bca.ac.uk

Tel: 01628 824444
Fax 01628 827488
• Beekeeping for beginners
• Practical Beekeeping
• Preparing Bees for Winter
• Intermediate Beekeeping
• Taster Sessions
• A Top up for beginners at the end of their first season
• Further techniques for more experienced beekeepers.

CHESHIRE BEEKEEPERS (STOCKPORT BRANCH)
• Introduction To Beekeeping Course,
• Practical Beekeeping,
Stockport :-
Mrs Carolin Hallworth
01625 875 436
North Cheshire (Frodsham):-
Dan Fox 01565 777 341

South Cheshire (Bradwall):-
Mrs Liz Camm 01270 664 337
Wirral
Doug Jones (Thornton Hough)
0151 342 7062

DEVON, Dr. Mick Street
c/o Bicton College
Budleigh Salterton
EX9 7BY
or the DBKA Education Officer at;
www.devonbeekeepers.co.uk

ESSEX, Richard Ridler
Treasurer,
C/O Saffron Walden Division,
Essex Beekeepers' Association,
Rundle House,
High Street
Hatfield Brand Oak,
Bishop's Stortford
Hertfordshire
CM22 7HE
richard.ridler@uwclub.net
01279 718111
07942 815753

LEEDS
For Details See YBKA

BCS

✉ ☎

BEEKEEPING EDITORS' EXCHANGE SCHEME

BEES is a self-help grouping of local, county and country beekeeping association editors, which operates principally by exchanging journals through a central address. The scheme is supported by Northern Bee Books.

BEES was founded in 1984 and for many years has been an exchange of paper copy. However, the focus has now changed to an electronic exchange, using the server of one of the participating editors.

Now fully established as part of the British and Irish beekeeping scene, the scheme brings up to date information to beekeepers throughout the British Isles.

The aims are:
- to exchange ideas for content and production methods
- to aid others by experience
- to communicate matters editorial
- to share information on national beekeeping issues
- to help and reassure those new to the task
- to give a wider readership to the best writing in beekeeping journalism

If you are an editor or potential editor and would like to know more about how we operate write to Martin Robinson.
The Manor House, Blackshaw Head, Hebden Bridge HX7 7JR
01422 - 842794

CONTACT,
Chris Jackson
22 Chapter Close
Oakwood
Derby
DE21 2BG

B.E.E.S
Helping Editors
Help Themselves

Sponsored by
NORTHERN BEE BOOKS

BEES ABROAD UK Ltd

Supporting beekeeping projects overseas

ADMINISTATOR
MRS JULES MOORE
PO BOX 2058
BRISTOL
BS35 9AF
0207 7193 7135
info@beesabroad.org.uk

Bees Abroad is a UK-registered charity (No 1108464) which was established in 1999. Its principle aim is the relief of poverty in the developing world using beekeeping and associated skills as a tool of individual, group and community empowerment for poverty alleviationand to provide sustainable income. Beekeeping is a valuable tool as it is socially and culturally acceptable for both genders across a wide age range.It can cost very little to set up a beekeeping operation, which will deliver benefits for income, education, health, environment and community. Beekeeping and its associated skills deliver access to gainful self-emplyment for poor and disadvantaged groups.   This enables them to recover social status, improve social interactions, obtain income and aquire new skills to build the confidence to represent their own interests. Bees Abroad receives a high volume of direct appeals for assistance from groups all over the world. In practice, it acheives its aims through a volunteer network of supporters, committee members and project managers.Bees Abroad takes care to ensure that its projects are sustainable and not dependent on constant external input. This is done by supporting community group initiatives, setting up village-based field extension services, running training courses for beekeeping trainers and financing local trainers' wages. All Bees Abroad projects are designed to become self-financing after a defines time period, usually 2-3 years, but sometimes longer. Its first two projects in Nepal and Cameroon now employ 42 beekeeper trainers and involve many more. It currently has projects either running or seeking funding in Malawi, Kenya, Ghana, Nepal, Uganda and Nigeria.

Our committee is almost entirely run by volunteers, who are all beekeepers. Volunteers and members currently undertake all activities, including fundraising, though a part-time administrator is employed for one day a week. We also arrange Beekeeping Holidays to variety of locations, including Chile, Cameroon and Kenya.
For more details of what we do and how you can help, you can contact Mrs Jules Moore the Administrator, Bees Abroad. Membership costs £15.00 per annum.

BFD

✉ ☎

BEES *for* DEVELOPMENT TRUST

Sustainable beekeeping. Poverty alleviation. Biodiversity.

www.beesfordevelopment.org

Bees *for* Development
PO Box 105,
Monmouth
NP25 9AA, UK
+44 (0) 1600713648
info@beesfordevelopment.org
UK Registered Charity
1078803

Beekeeping sustains the livelihoods of some of the poorest people in the world, and yet these communities lack the information and support they need to protect and advance their craft. Bees *for* Development provides advice, training and education to beekeepers in developing countries, helping them to earn more to pay for children' schooling and medical bills. Beekeeping is an effective way for beekeepers to create income from natural resources without damaging them, and supports biodiversity.

PLEASE SUPPORT BEES FOR DEVELOPMENT

- **SPONSOR** a Journal subscription for a beekeeper
- **MAKE** a gift of a *Resource Box* to a beekeeping club
- **GIVE** a donation or set up a *Direct Debit*
- **JOIN** one of our *Beekeepers' Safaris*
- **BUY** from our store: books, tamper proof seals
- **ATTEND** one of our *Courses*

Our work

Providing appropriate training and resources to improve understanding of apiculture and business

Publishing a regular journal for beekeepers in over 130 countries, provided free to those who need

Undertaking development projects with poor, rural communities, helping them to improve earnings

Advocating for enabling policies, ensuring that developing country beekeepers are given a voice

Advising and answering queries from 100s of beekeepers each month, giving expert advice to developing countries

BRITISH BEEKEEPERS'
ASSOCIATION www.bbka.org.uk

COMMITTEES OF THE EXECUTIVE AND SECRETARIES

FINANCE COMMITTEE
The Finance Committee reviews and agrees budgets and deals with issues relating to insurance, investments and setting the proposals for capitation etc. It acts as a co-ordinator for all external fund raising.

EDUCATION & HUSBANDRY
The Education and Husbandry Committee develops practical guidance on beekeeping, produces advisory leaflets on husbandry topics, liaises with the Examination Board to develop training materials to support Area Association tutors.

EXAMINATIONS BOARD
Secretary: Mrs Val Francis
val.francis@bbka.org.uk
The Examinations Board of the BBKA performs a national function, providing a structured range of examinations fulfilling the needs of all beekeepers. All matters concerning examinations, except for the correspondence course, should be addressed to the Examination Secretary.

PRODUCTS AND PROMOTIONS
The Products and Promotions Committee seeks ways to promote bees and beekeeping at both local and national level. It monitors media coverage and ensures that BBKA contributes to any relevant debate.

OPERATIONS DIRECTOR & GENERAL SECRETARY
Jane Moseley
The British Beekeepers' Association,
National Beekeeping Centre,
Stoneleigh Park
Warwickshire CV8 2LG
024 7669 6679
Fax: 024 7669 0682
Email:
jane.moseley@bbka.org.uk

BRITISH BEEKEEPERS ASSOCIATION
National Beekeeping Centre
Stoneleigh Park,
Kenilworth, Warks CV8 2LG
02476 696679
Fax: 024 7669 0682
Office hours 9.00am–5.00 pm
Monday - Friday (inclusive)
Telephone answering service outside office hours
Email:
bbka.info@bbka.org.uk
Web: www.bbka.org.uk

BBKA

⊠ ☎

EXECUTIVE COMMITTEE

PRESIDENT
Martin Smith
martin.smith@bbka.org.uk

CHAIRMAN
Brian Ripley
brian.ripley@bbka.org.uk

VICE CHAIRMAN
David Aston
david.aston@bbka.org.uk

TREASURER
Michael Sheasby
michael.sheasby@bbka.org.uk

ENVIRONMENTAL AND TECHNICAL

The Environmental and Technical Committee monitors technical developments and assesses their potential impact on bees and beekeeping.

SUBSCRIPTIONS AND MEMBERSHIP FEES

Individual membership fees for direct membership of the BBKA are now £25 for an overseas member or £33 per annum for UK members . All other membership is through local Area Associations.

LEGAL ADVICE

The Legal Adviser to the BBKA may be able to help Local Associations with legal problems to a limited extent. Contact through the NBC, BBKA, Stoneleigh Park, Kenilworth, CV8 2LG.

EVENTS

The various gatherings of beekeepers continue to be a feature of BBKA's many functions and provide a vital service for the dissemination of knowledge.

BBKA SPRING CONVENTION

The Spring Convention held in April is now a firmly established major event focussing on lectures, workshops and trade stands. Exhibition open on the Saturday to all.

OTHER NATIONAL EVENTS

The BBKA has stands featuring bees and promoting beekeeping at a number of national agricultural and garden shows throughout the year.

INSURANCE

Members and Area Associations and its Branches/ Divisions are indemnified against claims for Public Liability and Product Liability to a limit of £5 million. Each new claim carries an excess of £500 payable by the member.

Also available is the 'All Risks' Insurance for Associations which is available on request for use by Associations to cover the loss or damage to an Association's property or equipment. The terms of the policy are flexible and can be discussed with the broker.

Further details can be obtained from the BBKA Treasurer.

PUBLICATIONS
- The BBKA Year Book contains detailed information about the BBKA, including the Annual Accounts. Copies can may be purchased from the BBKA, Stoneleigh Park, Kenilworth, CV8 2LG or via the webshop at www.bbka.org.uk
- BBKA News is issued monthly and is free to all members of BBKA. The Editor is Mrs. S. Blake Email: editorial@bbkanews.org
- A Directory of Lecturers & Demonstrators is included in the Year Book.

BBKA ENTERPRISES LIMITED
BBKA Enterprises Ltd is a private company limited by guarantee with all profits from the trading activities being donated to the BBKA. The company offers a range of beekeeping, corporate and related items, specially selected gifts, travel items and educational material.
Visit the BBKA website for illustrations and details of prices. www.bbka.org.uk or contact BBKA Enterprises Ltd, NBC, Stoneleigh Park, Kenilworth, CV8 2LG Tel: 02476 696679.

BBKA WEBSITE - www.bbka.org.uk
The BBKA Website contains technical information, is easy to navigate and supports both beekeepers and the general public. You can download publications, find help and advice in the discussion forums, purchase merchandise, access the members' area, learn about Bees, use the Bees4kids section, download BBKA exam application forms and the exam syllabus.
Associations can promote their beekeeping events and have links to association websites.

BBKA

⊠ ☎

SLIDE AND VIDEO LIBRARY

A comprehensive catalogue of the BBKA Slide and VHS Video Library is available from Bridget Knutson, the Librarian at £4.50 including P&P. The slides are 35mm, both colour and B&W; some are supported with lecture notes. Many sets are now available as Power Point presentations, please enquire.

We are always pleased to receive suggestions for new additions to our range and for donations of items to improve the service. Please contact Mrs Bridget Knutson E mail: bridget_knutson@yahoo.co.uk

Examinations Footnote

Where Associations have no Examinations Secretary the Association Secretary deals with examinations. To help future candidates it is suggested that Associations without an Examination Secretary appoint one. Associations are responsible for arranging a suitable room for the written examinations and recommending an invigilator.

If you live in an area without a nominated Exam Secretary, you should contact Mrs Val Frances, Examinations Secretary, BBKA, NBC, Stoneleigh Park, Kenilworth, Warwickshire CV8 2LG
Email: Val.frances@bbka.org.uk Tel 01226 286341

✉ ☎

AREA ASSOCIATION SECRETARIES

AVON, Jane Godwin
Chatleigh house
6 Warminster Road
Limley Stoke
Bath
BA2 7GD
01225 723292
janegoodwin@macace.net

BERKSHIRE, Martin Moore,
19 Armour Hill
Tilehurst
READING
RG31 6JP
01189677386
07729620286
secretary.berksbees@
uwclub.net

BOURNEMOUTH
Mr A Curry
40 Lacy Drive,
Wimbourne, BW21 1DG
01202 840993
andrew@curry@virgin.net

BUCKS, Dr Beulah Cullen
26 Sweetcroft Lane,
Uxbridge, UB10 9LD,
01895 234704
beulah.cullen@virgin.net

CAMBRIDGESHIRE
Mrs Judith Evans MBE
7 The Furlongs
Needingworth
St Ives
Cambridgeshire PE27 4TX
01480 461203
judith@evans.cambnset.co.uk

CHESHIRE, M.F. Haynes
98, Gatley Road, Gatley,
Cheadle,
Cheshire SK8 4AB
0161 491 2382
thesecretary@cheshire-bka.
co.uk

CHESTERFIELD, Robin Bagnall
21 Ramper Avenue,
Clowne, Chesterfield
Derbyshire S43 4UD
01246 570545
ancient.mariner74-79@
virgin.net

CORNWALL, Julia Cooper
Whistow Farm, Lanlivery,
Bodmin, PL30 5DE
01208 872865
julia.i.cooper@btinternet.com

CORNWALL WEST
Mrs Berenice Robbins
Dr Anne McQuade,
5 Trevellan Road, Mylor
Bridge, Falmouth
Cornwall, TR11 5NE
01326 373749

CUMBRIA, Stephen C Barnes
8 Albemarle Street
Cockermouth
Cumbria CA13 0BG
01900 824872
braithwaitebees@sky.com

DERBYSHIRE, M J Cross
Harlestone, Beggarswell
Wood, Ambergate
Derbyshire DE56 2HF
01773 852772
crosssk@btinternet.com

DEVON, Andrew Kyle
62 Bicton Street,
Exmouth EX8 2RU
01395 263509
andrewkyle@tiscali.co.uk

DORSET, Mrs Ruth Homer
5, Malters Cottage,
Litton Cheney,
Dorchester DT2 9AE
beekeepers@hotmail.com

DOVER & DISTRICT
Mrs Maggie Harrowell
4 Harton Cottages, Ashley,
Dover, CT15 5HS
01304 821208
the.harrowells@btinternet.com

DURHAM, John Metson
7 Sidegate, Durham City,
Durham
0191 384 5170

ESSEX, Mrs Pat Allen
8 Frank's Cottages
St Mary's Lane
Upminster RM14 3NU
01708 220897
pat.allen@btconnect.com

GLOUCESTERSHIRE
Marie Toman
Oak Cottage,
Stoulgrove Lane, Woodcroft
Chepstow, Mon., NP16 7QE.
01291 620345
marietoman@btconnect.com

GWENT
Mrs J Bromley
Ty Hir, Monmouth Road
Raglan, Usk. NP15 2ET
01291 690331
bromleyjan@hotmail.com

BBKA

✉ ☎

HAMPSHIRE, Mrs P Barker
Brookdean, Hillbrow
Liss, Hampshire GU33 7PT
01730 895368
H'GATE & RIPON
Mr Frank Ward
19 High Street
Starbeck, Harrogate
HG2 7NS
01423 880266
HEREFORDSHIRE
Mrs. Wendy Cummins
Brook Cottage
Whitbourne
Worcsestershire WR6 5RT
01886 821485
jerryandwendy@btinternet.com
HERTFORDSHIRE
Luke Adams
53 Park Street Lane
Park Street
St. Albans
Hertfordshire AL2 2JA
01442 843 779
luke.skywalker@virgin.net
HUNTINGDON,
Nick Steiger
Bull Cottage, Main Street,
Upton, Huntingdon, Cambs,
PE28 5YB
01480 891935
n.steiger@btinternet.com
ISLE OF MAN,
Janet Thompson
Cott ny Greiney, The Smelt,
Beach Road, Port St Mary,
Isle of Man, IM9 5NF
01624 835524
jthompson@manx.net

ISLE OF WIGHT,
Mrs. Mary Case
Limerstone Farm
Limerstone,
Newport
Isle of White PO404AB
01983 759510
KENDAL &
SOUTH WESTMORLAND
Roger Blocksidge
Castle Garden Cottage
Aynam Road, Kendal
Cumbria LA9 7DE
01539 734436
tinky_winky@hotmail.com
KENT, John D. Hendrie
26 Coldharbour Lane
Hildenborough, Tonbridge
Kent TN11 9JT
01732 833894
jdh@bbka.freeserve.co.uk
LANCASHIRE & NORTH WEST
Martin Smith
137 Blaguegate Lane,
Lathom
Skelmersdale
Wigan WN8 8TX
05601 484388
ormskirk_beekeepers@
hotmail.com
LINCOLNSHIRE
Mrs. Celia Smith
Brookfield, Moor Town Road,
Nettleton LN7 6HX
01472 851165
LONDON
Nikki Vane
601 Alaska, 61 Grange Road
London SE1 3BB
07909 964986
sec@lbka.org.uk

LUDLOW & DIST
Andy M Vanderbrook
The Old Forge
Baveney Wood
Cleobury Mortimer
Kidderminster
DY14 8JD
01299 841379
andy.vanderhook@
care4free.net
MANCH. & DIST, Mrs. M. Bohme
54 Dunster Drive, Flixton
Manchester M41 6WR
0161 747 7292
MEDWAY Mrs. M. Pines
26 Lapwing Road
Isle of Grain, Rochester
ME3 0EB
01634 272252
MIDDLESEX, Mrs. J.V. Telfer
Midwood House
Elm Park Road
Pinner HA5 3LH
020 8868 3494
jvtelfer@hotmail.com
NEWCASTLE & DISTRICT,
Mr D Varty
Cragside, Dipton
Stan DH9 9EL
01207 570229
NORFOLK, Mrs H Coppwaite
1 The Maltings, Millgate
Aylsham, Norwich
NR11 6GX
01263 734682
NORFOLK WEST & KINGS LYNN
Mrs Irene Laws
16 Pine Road,
South Wootton
King's Lynn PE30 3JP
01553 671312

✉ ☎

NORTHAMPTONSHIRE
Mrs Ruth Stewart
17 Leys Avenue, Rothwell,
Kettering,
Northants, NN14 6JF
01536 507293
rstewart@euramax.co.uk
NORTHUMBERLAND
Mr Ben Hopkinson
11 Watershaugh Rd
Warkworth, Northumberland
NE65 0TT
01665 714213
benhopkinson2436@waitrose.
com
NOTTINGHAMSHIRE
M. Jordan
29 Crow Park Avenue
Sutton on Trent
Nr Newark NG23 6QG
01636 821613
mauricejordan11@btinternet.
com
OXFORDSHIRE, Mr Mark Lynch
71 Millwood End Long
Hanborough
Oxfordshire, OX 29 8BP
01993 883266
marka_lynch@hotmail.com
PETERBOROUGH & DISTRICT
P George Newton
65 Queen Street, Yaxley
Peterborough PE7 7JE
01733 243349
ROSELAND BEEKEEPING GROUP
Rose Hardisty
Menagwins Cottage,
Pentewan Road, St Austell,
Cornwall PL26 7AN
01726 74101
roselandbee@tiscali.co.uk

SEDBURGH
Jane Callus-Whitton
Harren House, Woodman
Lane, Cowan Bridge,
Carnforth, LA6 2HT
01524 272004
SHROPSHIRE
Mrs Penny Carkeet-James
Upper Dumble Holes
Westbury
Shrewsbury SY5 9HE
01743 791081
SHROPSHIRE NORTH
Mrs Jo Schup
Fields Farm, Malt Kiln Lane
Dobsons Bridge,
Whixall SY13 2QL
01948 720731
SOMERSET,
Mrs S Perkins
Tengore House,
Tengore Lane, Langport
Somerset TA10 9JL
01458 250095
bernieperkns.tengor@
tiscali.co.uk
STAFFORDSHIRE NORTH
Janey Hayward
90 Ostler's Lane
Cheddleton ST13 7HS
01538 361048
STAFFORDSHIRE SOUTH
Mr Steve Halford
46 Lincoln Hill Telford
TF8 7QA
01952 432031
stevehal@tiscali.co.uk

STRATFORD-ON-AVON
Michael Osborne
Oak Lodge, King's Lane
Snitterfield
Stratford-upon-Avon
Warwickshire CV37 0RB
01789 731745
mjroosborne@btinternet.com
SUFFOLK,
Ian McQueen
643 Foxhall Road
Ipswich IP3 8NE
01473 420187
jackie.mcqueen@ntlworld.com
SURREY, Mrs Sandra Rick
19 Kenwood Drive,
Walton-on-Thames
Surrey. KT12 5AU
01932 244 326
rickwoodsbka@googlemail.com
SUSSEX, Mrs Moyra Davidson
Gainsborough Cottage, Stunts
Green, Hertsmonceux,
East Sussex, BN27 4PN
01323 831 650
secretary@sussexbee.org.uk
SUSSEX WEST,
Mr John Glover
Fletchings Hollow
Vicarage Hill, Loxwood,
West Sussex RH14 0RJ
01403 751 899
glover.fletchershollow@
googlemail.com
THANET,
Mrs R Pearce
Summerfield Cottage
Summerfield
Woodnesborough
Nr Sandwich CT13 0EW
01304 614789

BBKA

✉ ☎

**TWICKENHAM & THAMES VALLEY
(MOLE APIARY CLUB)**
Mrs Sarah Crofton
11 Wellesley Avenue
London TW3 2PB
0208 222 8216
WARWICKSHIRE,
Theresa Simkin
87 Kineton Green Road
Solihull, B92 7DT
secretary@
warwickshirebeekeepers.org.uk

WILTSHIRE,
Ruth Woodhouse
Sandridge Tower
Bromham
Devizes
SN15 2JN
01225 705382
sandridgetower@aol.com
WORCESTERSHIRE
Mr Chris Broad, Upper
Gambolds Farm, Upper
Gambolds Lane, Stoke Prior,
B60 2DF
01527 872448

WYE VALLEY, Mrs S Wenczek
Hopleys, Bearwood
Leominster HR6 8EQ
01544 388302
YORKSHIRE, Brian Latham
111 Woodland Road
Whitkirk, Leeds
LS15 7DN
0113 264 3436
chrisbroad1964@btinternet.
com

ASSOCIATION EXAMINATION SECRETARIES

AVON, Position Vacant
Please contact
Hon. General Secretary
Julie Young
01179 372 156
BERKSHIRE,
Mrs Rosemary Bayliss
Norbury, Coppid Beech Hill,
Binfield, Berkshire.
RG42 4BS
01344 421747
BOURNEMOUTH, Mrs. M. Davies
80 Leybourne Avenue
Ensbury Park
Bournemouth
Dorset BH10 6HE
01202 526077

BUCKS, John Chudley
Orchard Lea, Oxford Street
Lea Common
Great Missenden HP16 9JT
01494 837544
jlchudley@tiscali.co.uk
CHESHIRE
Graham Royle NDB,
7, Symondley Road,
Sutton,
Macclesfield. SK11 0HT
01260 252 042
CORNWALL
Mrs. Susan Malcolm
Fig Tree, 333 New Road
Saltash, Cornwall
PL12 6HL
01752 845496

DEVON, Roger Lacey
Gatchell House
Toadpit Lane, Ottery St Mary
Devon EX11 1TR
01404 811733
devonbees@pobox.com
DORSET, K.G.Bishop
72 Alexandra Road
Bridport DT6 5AL
01308 425479
DURHAM, G. Eames
23 Lancashire Drive
Belmont, Durham,
DH1 2DE
01913 845220
george.eames@durham.ac.uk

ESSEX, Pat Allan
8, Frank's Cottages
St. Mary's Lane
Upminster, RM14 3NU
pat.allen@btconnect.com

GLOUCESTERSHIRE
Bernard Danvers
120a Ruspidge Road
Cinderford,
Glocestershire
GL143AG
01594 825063

GWENT, Mrs J Bromley
Ty Hir, Monmouth Road
Raglan, Usk. NP15 2ET
01291 690331
bromleyjan@hotmail.com

HAMPSHIRE, Mrs Peggy Mason
37 Springford Crescent
Lordswood,
SO16 5LF
023 8077 7705

H'GATE & RIPON, Peter Ross
The Wheelhouse, The Green,
Old Scriven, Knaresborough
HG5 9EA, 01423 866565,
pjeross@btinternet.com

HEREFORDSHIRE, Len J. Dixon
The Square, Titley,
Kington
Herefordshire HR5 3RG
01544 230884
beeline2ljd@yahoo.co.uk

HERTFORDSHIRE, R. E. A. Dartington
15 Benslow Lane
Hitchin SG4 9RE
01462 450707
gray.dartington@dial.pipex.com

ISLE OF WIGHT, Mrs M. Case
Limerstone Farm,
Limerstone, Newport,
Isle of Wight, PO30 4AB
01983 740223
gcase90337@aol.com

KENT, P. F. W. Hutton
22 Good Station Road
Tunbridge Wells,
TN1 2DB
01892 530688

LANCASHIRE & NW
Edward Hill
3 Sandy Lane, Aughton
Ormskirk
L39 6SL
01695 423137

LEICESTERSHIRE & RUTLAND
Brian Cramp
2 Woodland Drive, Groby
Leicester
LE6 0BQ
01162 876879

LINCOLNSHIRE, R. J. B. Hickling
Linden Lea, Sandbraes
Lane, Caistor, LN7 6SB
01472 851473

MIDDLESEX
Mrs Jo V Telfer
Midwood House
Elm Park Road, Pinner
Middlesex HA5 3LH
020 8868 3494
e-mail, jvtelfer@hotmail.com

NOTTINGHAMSHIRE
Dr Glyn D Flowerdew
Knight Cross Cottage
Newstead Abbey Park
Ravenshead
Nottinghamshire NG15 8GE
01623 792812

OXFORDSHIRE, Terry. Thomas
4 Kirk Close
Oxford, OX2 8JN
01865 558679

PETERBOROUGH, P. G .Newton
65 Queen Street, Yaxley
Peterborough PE7 3JE
01733 243349

SHROPSHIRE NORTH
Paul Curtis
1 Hammer Close
Overton-on-Dee, Wrexham
Clwyd LL13 0LD0
01691 624296

SOMERSET, Mrs Angela Bache
Greenway House
Badgers Cross
Somerton TA11 7JB
Tel 01458 273149

STAFFS.Nth Dr. Nick C Mawby
Glenwood, Wood Lane
Longsdon,
Stoke on Trent ST9 9QB
01538 387506
info@northstaffsbees.org.uk

STAFFS. SOUTH
Tony Burton
96 Weeping Cross, Stafford,
Staffordshire. ST9 9QB
01538 399322

SUFFOLK, Mr Ian McQueen
643 Foxhall Road, Ipswich,
Suffolk, IP3 8NE
01473 420187

SURREY, Mrs. A. Gill
143 Smallfield Road
Horley, RH6 9LR
01293 784161

SUSSEX, Nigel Champion
45 Ridgeway,
Hurst Green
Etchingham
East Sussex TN19 7PJ
01580 860379

SUSSEX WEST
Mrs A. S. Gibson-Poole
Mont Dore, West Hill
High Salvington
Worthing, BN13 3BZ
01903 260914

BBKA

Where Associations have no Examinations Secretary the Association Secretary deals with examinations. To help future candidates it is suggested that Associations without an Examination Secretary appoint one. Associations are responsible for arranging a suitable room for the written examinations and recommending an invigilator.

If you live in an area without a nominated Exam Secretary, you should contact Mrs Val Frances, 39 Beevor Lane, Gawber, Barnsley, S75 2RP Tel 01226 286341. e-mail, valfrances@blueyonder.co.uk

HOLDERS OF THE BBKA SENIOR JUDGES CERTIFICATE

ASHLEY, Mr. T. E.
Meadow Cottage
Elton Lane, Winterley
Sandbach
Cheshire CW11 4TN
BADGER, M.J , MBE
14 Thorn Lane
Leeds, LS8 1NN
BLACKBURN, Mrs. H.M
15 Highdown Hill Road
Emmer Green
Reading RG4 8QR
BROWN, Mrs. V
BUCKLE, M.J
The Little House
Newton Blossomville
Bedford MK43 8AS
01234 881262
martin@newtonbee.fsnet.
co.uk
CAPENER, Rev. H.F.
1 Baldric Road
Folkestone CT20 2NR
COLLINS, G.M. , NDB
72 Tatenhill Gardens
Doncaster DN4 6TL
COOPER, Miss R.M
10 Gaskells End
Tokers Green
Reading RG4 9EW
DAVIES, Mrs. M
80 Leybourne Avenue
Ensbury Park
Bournemouth BH10 6HE

DIAPER, B
B Diaper
57 Marfield Close
Walmley
West Midlands
0121 313 3112
or 07711 456932
DICKSON, Ms. F
Didlington Manor
Didlington, Thetford
Norfolk IP26 5AT
DUFFIN, J.M
Upper Hurst
Salisbury Road, Blashford
Ringwood
Hampshire BH24 3PB
01425 474552
DUGGAN, R.M
Redstone Wood Cottage
Philanthropic Lane
Redhill RH1 4DF
FIELDING, L.G
Linley, Station Road
Lichfield WS13 6HZ
MacGIOLLA COSA, M.C.
Glengarra Wood, Burncourt
Cahir, Co. Tipperary
Republic of Ireland
McCORMICK, E.
14 Akers Lane, Eccleston St.
Helens, Lancs WA10 4QL
MOXON, G
9 Savery Street
Southcoates Lane
Hull HU9 3BG

ORTON J
Occupation Road, Sibson
Nuneaton CV13 6LD
ROUNCE J.N , NDB
4 Scarborough Road
Great Walsingham
NR22 6AB
SALTER T.A , MBE
44 Edward Road, Clevedon
North Somerset BS21 7DT
SYMES, C.J
189 Marlow Bottom Road
Marlow SL7 3PL
TAYLOR, A.J
The Old Pyke Cottage
Hethelpit Cross, Staunton
GL19 3QJ
VICKERY, R.G.L
Ponderosa, Verwood Road
Three Legged Cross
Wimborne BH21 6RN
WILLIAMS, M
Tincurry, Cahir,
Co Tipperary, Eire
YOUNG, M
Mileaway, Carnreagh
Hillsborough,
Northern Island BT26 6LJ

BIBBA

⊠ ☎

BEE IMPROVEMENT & BEE BREEDERS' ASSOCIATION

www.bibba.com

SECRETARY
Pam Hunter
Burnthouse,
Burnthouse Lane,
Cowfold, Horsham,
West Sussex, RH13 8DH.
01403 864007
pamhunter@burnthouse.org.uk

BIBBA is an organisation devoted to encouraging beekeepers to breed native bees. The bee more suited to our environmental circumstances than other sub species. BIBBA's aims are publicised through books, workshops, lectures and conferences.

BIBBA also co-operates with worldwide Beekeeping and breeding groups interested in conserving and improving their own native bees.

MEMBERSHIP SECRETARY
David Allen
75 Newhall Road,
Doncaster. DN3 1QQ
01302 88581350
membership@bibba.com

Breeding techniques advocated include:
• Assessment of colonies by observation, recording certain criteria on standard record cards.
• Determination and purity of sub species by measurement of morphometric characters and mitrochondial DNA.
• Use of mini nucs for the mating of queens economically

SALES SECRETARY
John Hendrie
26 Coldharbour Lane
Hildenborough
Tonbridge
Kent
TN11 9JT
sales@bibba.com

BIBBA Publications include:
• The Honeybees of the British Isles by Beowulf Cooper
• Breeding Techniques and Selection for Breeding of the Honeybee by Prof. F. Ruttner
• The Dark European Honey Bee by Prof. F. Ruttner, Rev. Eric Milner and John Dews
• Breeding Better Bees using Simple Modern Methods by John E. Dews and Rev.Eric Milner
• Better Beginnings for Beekeepers by Adrian Waring - second edition.

BIBBA encourages the formation of Bee Breeding Groups, and the sharing of knowledge between groups by the provision of genetic material.
Look out for Queen Rearing events in the bee press and on www.bibba.com.

CBDBBRT

THE C.B. DENNIS BRITISH BEEKEEPERS' RESEARCH TRUST

REGISTERED CHARITY NO. 328685

Aims

This Charitable Trust was established in 1990 through the generosity of Mr C.B. Dennis. It aims to support research at institutions or by individuals and to encourage young scientists through the provision of grants for agreed projects and broader bee science that benefit bees and beekeeping in Britain.

Awards

The Trust is administered by a group of Trustees, most of whom have relevant scientific, environmental or ecological expertise that helps to ensure that work funded by the Trust is properly evaluated and provides the greatest possible advantage for bees.

Since its inception the Trust has funded work on a wide range of topics related to both honey bees and other bees. Grants have been made, for example, for work on: bee pathogens, pollination and broader ecological concepts. Work is not limited to the UK and research at European universities and laboratories may also be funded.

Young scientists have been supported through studentships and applications for such research bursaries are invited.

Donations

The Trust is pleased to acknowledge the loyal support it already receives from several local beekeeping associations and many individuals. All donations, however small, will be added to the invested capital and bee research in Britain will benefit from the income in perpetuity.

Full details of the activities of the Trust, outputs of the research funded and grant application forms can be obtained from www.cbdennistrust.org.uk

CABK

✉ ☎

THE CENTRAL ASSOCIATION OF BEEKEEPERS

www.cabk.org.uk

SECRETARY, Pat Allen
8 Frank's Cottages
St Mary's Lane
Upminster, RM14 3NU

PRESIDENT, Prof. R.S. Pickard
Consumer's Association
2 Marylebone Rd
London, NW1 4DF

TREASURER, John Hendrie
26 Coldharbour Lane
Hildeborough
Tonbridge, TN11 9JT

PROGRAMME SECRETARY
Pam Hunter
Burnthouse
Burnthouse Lane
Cowfold, Horsham
RH13 8DH

EDITOR, Pat Allen
8, Frank's Cottages
St. Mary's Lane
Upminster, RM14 3NU

SALES AND DISTRIBUTION,
Margaret Thomas
The Battinbuin Bothy
Battinbuin, Strathtay,
Pitlochy, PH9 0LP

The Central Association of Beekeepers in its present form dates from the time of the reorganisation of the British Beekeepers' Association in 1945. The BBKA was originally made up of private members only. However as County Associations were formed they applied for affiliation and were later permitted to send delegates to meetings of the Central Association, as the private members were then known. This arrangement became unsatisfactory as the voting power of the Central Association greatly outnumbered that of the County Associations and so in 1945 a new Constitution was drawn up whereby the Council comprised Delegates from the Counties and Specialist Member Associations. The private members then formed themselves into a Specialist Member Association with the designation 'The Central Association of the British Beekeepers' Association'; this was later shortened to its present style.

The Association was able to devote itself to its own particular aims, to promote interest in current thought and findings about beekeeping and aspects of entomology related to honey-bees and other social insects. Lectures given by scientists and other specialists are arranged, printed and circulated to members, as has been done since 1879.

An annual Spring Conference is held in London and an Autumn Conference in the Midlands. In addition, a lecture is presented at the Annual General Meeting and at the Social Evening held during the National Honey Show. The subscription is £10.00 per annum, £12.00 for dual membership (one copy only of publications).

BEE MAGS

COUNTY BEEKEEPING MAGAZINES AND NEWSLETTERS

AVON, Ms Julie Young
1 Church Cottages
Abson Road, Abson Wick
Bristol, BS30 5TT
0117 937 2156
julieyoung@btinternet.com
BEDFORDSHIRE, Sue Lang
154a Lower Shelton
Road, Upper Shelton
Marston Moretaine
Beds, MK43 0LS
01234 764180
07879 848550
bedfordshirehoney@hotmail.co.uk
BERKSHIRE, Ron Crocker
25 Ship Lake Bottom
Peppard Common
Oxon RG9 5HH
CAMBRIDGESHIRE, Mr. Chris Evans
7 The Furlongs,
Needingworth,
St. Ives,
Cambs. PE27 4TX
CHESHIRE, Pete Sutcliffe
2 Hatfield Court
Holmes Chapel,
Cheshire, CW4 7HP
h.p.sutcliffe@googlemail.com.

CHESTERFIELD & DISTRICT Mrs Margaret Edge
4 Cinder Hill,
Shireoaks,
Worksop, S81 8NR
CORNWALL, Gillian Searle
6 Harleigh Road, Bodmin
Cornwall PL31 1AQ
CUMBRIA, Dave Bates
Greenfield House
Low Green
Temple Sowerby
Penrith CA10 1SD
DERBYSHIRE, Mrs. M. Cowley
14 Montpelier, Quorndon
Derby DE22 5JW
DEVON, Glyn R Davies
Landscore
Eastern Rd, Ashburton
Devon TQ13 7AR
01364 652640
landscore@eclipse.co.uk
DORSET, Mrs L Gasson
The White House,
Candy's Lane,
Shilllingstone. DT11 0SF
01258 861690
DURHAM, George Eames
11, Sharon Avenue,
Kelloe, Durham DH6 4NE
07970 926250
beeseames@btinternet.com

ESSEX, Pat Allen
8 Franks Cottages
St Mary's Lane
Upminster RM14 3NU
GLOUCESTERSHIRE, Mrs A Ellis
19 Whaddon Road
Cheltenham
Gloucestershire GL52 5LZ
GUERNSEY BKA Ruth Collins
Colombier House
Torteval
Guernsey GY8 0NF
GWENT, Keith Allen
Pen-y-Lan Cottage,
Far Hill, Trellech,
Monmouth, NP25 4PP
kh.allen@virgin.net
HAMPSHIRE, Dr Helen Harley Communications Manager
Programme Management
Unit (PMU)
University of
Southampton
Bassett House
Chetwynd Road
Southampton SO16 3TU
023 8059 2804
HEREFORDSHIRE, Mr. Len Dixon
The Square,
Titley Kington, HR5 3RG
beeline2ljd@yahoo.co.uk

BEE MAGS

HERTFORDSHIRE
Paul Cooper
01279 771231
HUNTINGDON
Wilma Vaughan
Lauriston Copse
Warboys, Huntingdon
Cambs PE28 2US
KENDAL & SOUTH
WESTMORLAND
Roger Blocksidge
20 Fowl Ing Lane
Kendal
Cumbria
LA9 6HB
tinky_winky@
hotmail.com
KENT,John Hendrie
26, Coldharbour
Lane,Hildenborough,
Tonbridge Kent
TN11 9JT
LEEDS BEEKEEPER
Editor Bill Cadmore,
104 Hall Lane
Horsforth, Leeds
LS18 5JG
0113 2160482
leeds.
bill.cadmore@
ntlworld.com
LEICS. & RUTLAND
Editor, T. Strachan
54 Burgess Rd.
Coalville,
Leicestershire LE67 3PX
terry@trs-net.co.uk

LINCOLNSHIRE, P. Raines
Grange Cottage
21 Humberston Av.
Humberstone
Grimsby DN36 4SL
LONDON, Steve Bembow
156 D evon Mansions
Tooley Street
London SE1 2NR
MEDWAY, Rob Smith
robert_787@hotmail.
com
MOLE A. CLUB,
Dennis Cutler
70 Hurst Road
East Molesey
Surrey KT8 9AG
NEWCASTLE, George Batey
Rift Farm Cottage
Wylam NE41 8BL
NORFOLK, Michael Lancefield
Candlemas House
Fakenham Road
Stanhoe
King's Lynn PE31 8PX
lancefield@aol.com
NOTHAMPTONSHIRE
Roger G Virgo
5 Surfleet Close, Corby
Northamptonshire
NN18 9BG
amellifera@aol.com
NOTTINGHAMSH,
Stuart Ching
122 Marshall Hill Drive
Porchester
Notts NG3 6HW

SOMERSET, Richard Bache
The Annex,
Moorview Farm
Midelney Road
Drayton, Near langport
Somerset, TA10 0LW
newsletter@somerset
beekeepers.org.uk
SUFFOLK, Tony Molesworth
Kizimbani, Bildeston
Road, Combs. IP14 2JZ
tony.molesworth@essex.
businesslink.co.uk
WARWICKSHIRE, Rob Jones
124 Ashfurlong Road
Sutton Coldfield
B75 6EW
0121 378 0562
wbeditor@warwickshire-
beekeepers.org.uk
WILTSHIRE,
Ronald A Hoskins,
10 Larksfield
Covingham Park
Swindon SN3 5AD
WORCESTER,
Mrs U Brandwood
10 Monnow Close
Droitwich
Worcester WR9 8T
Ursula@brandwoodu.
freeserve.co.uk
YORKSHIRE
Newsletter Editor,
Bill Cadmore,
104 Hall Lane, Horsforth
Leeds LS18 5JG
0113 216 0482
bill.cadmore@
ntlworld.com

CONBA UK, COUNCIL OF THE NATIONAL BEEKEEPING ASSOCIATIONS IN THE UNITED KINGDOM

CONBA was established in 1978 to promote the aims and objectives of the national beekeeping associations of England, Scotland, Ulster and Wales. Its purpose is to represent the interests of beekeepers' with local, national and international authorities. A representative delegate from each of the member country associations occupies the chair for a period of two years, on a rotational basis.

The council meets twice per year, normally at Stoneleigh and at the National Honey Show in London, with the remaining meeting by rotation in the member association's country. Council business consists of any matters of common interest to all its members.

CONBA provides representation of its membership at the European Union (EU) through two specific committees, COPA and COGECA (COPA – Comite des Organisations Professionelles Agricoles de la CEE); (COGECA Comite de la Cooperation Agricole de la CEE); and the Honey Working Party (HWP).

The Honey Working Party meetings are held at Brussels. This committee liases with the European Commission in relation to apicultural matters concerning the member states of the European Union (EU). These matters are subsequently presented to the European Parliament for its consideration, implementation or revision or rejection. The subsequent approval of such matters results in establishing legislation, government support and possible EC funding relating to the practice of apicultural production in the UK through its membership of the EU.

INCORPORATING THE BEEKEEPING ORGANISATIONS OF:
England, Channel Islands Isle of Man, Scotland, Ulster, Wales

SECRETARY
Terry Gibson. MSc.
17 Ffolkes Drive,
Gaywood,
King's Lynn, Norfolk.
PE30 3BX.
01553 674051
bee-aware@gmx.com

CHAIRMAN, Dinah Sweet
Graigfawr Lodge,
Caerphilly CF83 1NF
sweetd@cardiff.ac.uk

VICE-CHAIRMAN, Mervyn Eddie
eddie_mervyn@yahoo.co.uk

HON. TREASURER, Martin Tovey
11, Coach Road,
Carnforth, Lancashire,
LA5 9PP.
martintovey@hotmail.co.uk

CONBA
✉ ☎

DARG

DEVON APICULTURAL
RESEARCH GROUP

DARG is an independent group of experienced enthusiastic beekeepers whose primary aim is to collect and analyse data on matters of topical interest which may assist their apicultural education and promote the advancement of beekeeping. At their monthly meetings, DARG members discuss various topics in open forum, during which they exchange ideas and information from their personal beekeeping knowledge and experience. They also undertake suitable research projects which further the Group's aims.

TOPICS CURRENTLY BEING UNDERTAKEN
• Use of Shook Colonies and Comb Change in the control of brood diseases.
• Methods of Integrated Pest Management for the control of varroa.
• Honeybee genetics with particular reference to the selection of breeder queens.
• A survey of Useful bee plants, shrubs and trees in the South West.

PUBLICATIONS AVAILABLE
• **The Beeway Code.** A common sense guide for beginners to help avoid problems with neighbours and produce a safe and peaceful apiary.
• **Seasonal Management.** A useful aid to planning your work effectively
• **Living with Varroa jacobsoni.** A best selling title and an invaluable weapon in winning the war against the mite - updated in 1999
• **Queen Rearing.** Providing detailed help in rearing new queens in order to promote vigorous colonies.
• **Selection of Apiary Sites** full of tips for choosing the right sites for your bees.

CHAIRMAN, Richard Ball
Stoneyford Farmhouse
Colaton Raleigh
Sidmouth
Devon EX10 0HZ
HON SECRETARY, Kingsley Law
Halwell Farm, Denbury
Newton Abbot, TQ12 6ED
0180 381 2285

PUBLICATIONS OFFICER, David Loo
25 Woodlands
Newton-St-Cyres, Exeter
Devon EX5 5BP
0139 285 1472

TREASURER, Bob Ogden
Pennymoor Cottage
Pennymoor
Tiverton
Deven EX16 8LJ
01363 866687

All titles cost £2.50 per copy (post free) from the Publications Officer (tel. 01392 851472). Discounts are available for BBKA affiliated Associations **Please contact the Publications Officer for details**

139

EAS

✉ ☎

THE EASTERN APICULTURAL SOCIETY OF NORTH AMERICA

www.easternapiculture.org

Kathy Summers, 623 West Liberty Street, Medina Ohio 44256
Kathy@BeeCulture.com

The Eastern Apicultural Society of North America (www.easternapiculture.org) holds their annual Short Course and Conference each Summer during July or August. In 2012 EAS will be held at the University of Vermont in Burlington, August 13-17, hosted by the Vermont Beekeepers Association with Bill Mares acting as president.

The week starts with a two-day Short Course with an advanced level and a beginning level – something for everyone. This is a fairly intense classroom setting with beeyard activities, focused on increasing your knowledge and ability as a beekeeper. Then on Wednesday the Main Conference begins with lectures and on Thursday and Friday workshops in the afternoon on every topic you can imagine. We offer workshops on beekeeping and many related activities – some years cooking with honey, soap making, candle making – so much you can't possibly see and hear it all.

In 2013 EAS will be in Pennsylvania and moving forward we're hoping to be in Kentucky in 2014. So please visit our website – www.easternapiculture.org – watch for details of upcoming conferences. We will have our program, speakers and other activities listed just as soon as it is set.

If you have questions or want more information you can also contact Kathy Summers, EAS Vice Chairman of EAS, kathy@beeculture.com.

FIBKA

THE FEDERATION OF IRISH BEEKEEPERS' ASSOCIATIONS

http://www.irishbeekeeping.ie

Comhnascadh Cumann Beachairí na hEireann

ANNUAL SUMMER COURSE

The 2010 Beekeeping Summer Course held at the Franciscan College, Gormanston, Co Meath will take place from 26th of July to Saturday 31st July 2010. Guest Speaker will be Mr Dewey Caron from the University of Delaware, America. Dewey is Professor of Entomology & Applied Ecology at the College of Agricultural & National Resources at the University of Delaware, USA.

Full course including accommodation and meals €310. For reservation, send deposit of €40 to Summer Course Convenor: Mr Gerry Ryan, Deerpark, Dundrum, Co Tipperary (062-71274) or Email ryansfancy@gmail.com

PUBLICATIONS

- **Beekeeping in Ireland - A History** - J.K. Watson

This book gives the history of the craft from time immemorial to the present. It is well bound, hard backed and excellently presented. There are 293 pages of valuable information and 53 pictures of prominent beekeepers past and present. Price €7.00

- **Bees, Hives and Honey** - Published by F.I.B.K.A. - Edited by Eddie O'Sullivan.

This book has been compiled from writings by some of Ireland's most prominent beekeepers of the present day. It is an instruction book on beekeeping published as a millennium project and should prove a modern treatise on the craft of beekeeping and its associated products. There are over 200 pages, also many photographs and illustrations. Price €12.70 (Paperback) or €19 (Hardback)

Available from Eddie O'Sullivan, Phone: 021-4542614, Email : eosbee@indigo.ie

---

HON. SECRETARY
Mr. Michael G. Gleeson
Ballinakill Enfield Co. Meath
046 9541433
e-mail, mgglee@eircom.net

PRESIDENT
Mr Dennis Ryan
Mylerstown, Clonmel, Co
Tipperary, 052 25600
Email dryan266@eircom.net

VICE PRESIDENT
Mr Seamus Reddy
8 Tower View Park, Kildare,
045 521945
Email
seamusreddy@eircom.net

PRO Mr P.McCabe,
"Sherdara"
Beuaulieu Cross
Drogheda, Co. Louth
041 983 6159
philipmccabe@eircom.net
HON. EDITOR, Jim Ryan
Innisfail, Kickham Street
Thurles, Co Tipperary
0504 22228
jimbee1@eircom.net

FIBKA

✉ ☎

HON. MANAGER, Mr. David Lee
Scart, Kildorry, Co. Cork
022 25595
davidleej@eircom.net

HON. TREASURER,
Mrs Bridie Terry
"Ait na Greine", Coolbay
Cloyne, Midleton,Co Cork
0214652141
aitnagreine@gmail.com

EDUCATION OFFICER
Dr. Brendan Coughlan
Ard na gCloch, Corcullen
Moycullen, Co. Galway
091 555211
B.OCochlain@irishbroad-
band.net

LIBRARIAN Jim Ryan.
Innisfail, Kickham Sr
Thurles,co Tipperary
jimbee1@eircom.net

SUMMER COURSE CONVENER
Mr Gerry Ryan
Deerpark, Dundrum,
Co Tipperary
062 71274
ryansfancy@gmail.com

HONEY SHOW SECRETARY
Mr R Williams
Tincurry
Cahir
Co Tipperary, Eire
052 7442617
emwilliams@eircom.net

- **The Irish Bee Guide** - Reverend J.D. Dgges
First published in 1904, It was proclaimed as an excellent book on beekeeping. It also won a place as a notable production in the literary context. It eventually ran to sixteen editions and sold seventy-six thousand copies overall. The name was changed in the second issue to The Practical Bee Guide. Now, one hundred years later, a decision has been taken to honour this great work. What better way to do it than to re-issue the book as it was in 1904 when it first entered the literary world. The re-print is an exact replica of the original first edition. The price per copy is Hardback €30 and Softback €20
Available from Eddie O'Sullivan, Phone : 021-4542614, Email: eosbee@indigo.ie

- **An Beachaire** - The Irish Beekeeper
the monthly organ of FIBKA, subscription £20.00 Stg post free from The Manager. Readership of the Journal in Northern Ireland carries third party insurance public liability cover up to €6.500,000 on any one claim and product liability cover up to €6.500,000 on any one claim, on payment of £5.00 Stg extra.

LIBRARY
The library is owned and controlled by FIBKA. It contains very many valuable books ancient and modern, available to members for return postage only. The Librarian is Jim Ryan, Innisfail, Kickham Street, Thurles, Co Tipperary.
Email: jimbee1@eircom.net

CORRESPONDENCE COURSES
The Examination Board has sponsored correspondence courses for candidates preparing for the Intermediate and Senior (Bee Masters) Examinations. Applications to John Cunningham, Ballygarron, Kilmeaden, Co Waterford, Tel No 051-399897/086-8399108 Email: john3cunningham@hotmail.com

EXAMINATIONS
The Board conducts five grades of examinations at the annual Summer Course at Gormanston College: Preliminary, Intermediate, Senior, Lecturer and Honey Judge. Preliminary and Intermediate Examinations are also held at Provincial centres in May each year.

EDUCATION
The Federation Examinations are recognised as Third Level Examinations by the National Council for Educational Awards (NCEA), thus candidates who pass the Senior Examination may apply to the NCEA for a National Certificate in Science (Apiculture) and candidates who have passed the Lectureship

Examination and who have at least two years' experience as Lecturers and who have also gained a sufficient standing in the beekeeping community may apply to the NCEA for a Diploma in Science (Apiculture), these awards are conferred by the Cork Institute of Technology (CIT) under a programme of Experiential Learning, for the Diploma a comprehensive Portfolio must be submitted to CIT, successful candidates are entitled to use the qualification NatDipSc (Apic).

Courses for beginners are run by Affiliated Associations and the FIBKA holds an Annual Summer Course in Gormanston College in July. The course caters for the three grades of students: beginners, intermediate, and senior and covers the theory and practice of modern apiculture. Examinations are held in these grades and also at Honey Judge and Lecturer level. Further information on the Examinations may be obtained from the Education Officer, Dr Brendan Coughlan, Chemistry Department, National University of Ireland, Galway (e-mail : B.OCochlain@irishbroadband.net)

NATIONAL HONEY SHOW

This is held at Gormanston College in conjunction with the annual Beekeeping Course. The Schedule contains 32 Open Classes and 3 Confined classes with €1,000 in prizes. Over 30 Challenge Cups and Trophies are presented for the competition.

Honey Show Secretary: Mr Redmond Williams, Tincurry, Cahir, Co Tipperary Tel No 052-7442617 e-mail: emwilliams@eircom.net

INSURANCE

The limit of indemnity of public liability policy is €6.500,000 arising from one accident or series of accidents. There is also product liability of €6.500,000 arising from any one claim. The policy extends to all registered affiliated members whose subscriptions are fully paid up on the 31st December of any one year and whose names are entered in the FIBKA register held by the Treasurer.

LIFE VICE PRESIDENTS

Mr. M.I Moynihan
41 Caseyville, Dungarvan
Co. Waterford
058 42389
Mr. P. O'Reilly
11 Our Lady's Place,
Naas Co. Kildare
045 897568
Mr. M.L. Woulfe
Railway House, Midleton
Co. Cork
021 631011
Mrs Frances Kane
Firmount, Clane,
Co Kildare,
087 2450640
or 045 893150

ASSOCIATION SECRETARIES

ASHFORD, Mr Michael Giles
55 Saunders Lane, Rathnew,
Co Wicklow
086-8369152
BANNER,Ms Aoife Nic Giolla
Blossom Lodge, Derra,
Kilkisken, Co Clare.
087 6743030
CARBERY, MrSean O'Donovan
Drominidy, Drimologue
Co Cork, 087 7715001
CARLOW, Mr. John Lennon
31 Idrone Park, Tullow Road,
Carlow   059 9141315

CO. CAVAN, Ms Christine Grey
Tullyvin, Cootehill, Co Craven
049 5553164
CO. CORK, Mr Robert McCutcheon
Clancoolemore, Bandon,
Cork. 023-41714
CO. DONEGALMr Derek Byrne
Carrick West, Laghey
Co.Donegal
074 9722340
CO. DUBLIN, Mr Liam McGarry
24 Quinns Road, Shankill,
Co Dublin.
087-2643492

CO. GALWAY,
Dr. Brendan Coughlan
Ard na gCloch, Corcullen,
Galway
091 555211
CO. KERRY, Mr Ruary Rudd
Westgate, Waterville,
Co. Kerry
066 9474251
CO. LIMERICK, Mr. Sean Flavin
Creeves Cross,
Shanagolden, Co. Limerick
069 60328

FIBKA

✉ ☎

CO. LOUTH,
Ms Patricia Finlay Hanratty
Grey Acre, Kilkerley,
Dundalk, Co Louth.
042-9329153 or 087-0640413

CO. LONGFORD,
Mrs Brigit Koston
Sunnyside House
Loughgowna, Co. Cavan
043 83285

CO. MAYO Mrs. Cathy Dunne,
Cloofinish, Swinford,
Co. Mayo 094 9252543

CO. OFFALY,
Mr Cyril Page
Woodford, Loughrea,
Co Galway.
0906-749025/086-8043072

CO. WATERFORD
Mr Pat Dillane,
Coolbagh, Clashmore,
Co. Waterford
02496979

CO. WEXFORD
Mr. Padraig McKenna
Blake Cottage, Curracloe,
Co. Wexford

DUNHALLOW,
Mr Andrew Bourke,
Pallas, Lombardstown,
Mallow, Co Cork
087 2783807

DUNAMAISE,
Mr Seamus Brennan
Bondra,Colt,
Ballyroan, Co Laois
057 8731871

DUNMANWAY,
Mr. Michael I O'Sullivan
Ballyhalwick Dunmanway,
Co. Cork (023) 45257

EAST CORK, Mr C Terry
"Ait na Graine", Coolbay
Cloyne, Co. Cork
021 4652141

EAST WATERFORD
Mr. Michael Hughes
51 Woodlawn Grove

Cork St, Waterford
051 373461

FINGAL, Mr John McMullan
34 Ard na Mara Crescent
Malahide, Co. Dublin
(01) 8450193

FOYLE, P J Costello
Lr Drumaiveir, Greencastle
Co Donegal
074 9381303

GOREY, Mr Joe Nealon
Aspen Woods,
Raheenteigue, Tinahely,
Co Wicklow.
0402-38481

INNISHOWEN,
Mr Paddy McDonagh,
Milltownwn, Carndonagh
Co. Donegal 074 9374881

KILLORGLIN, Mr Mike Cronin
Upper Tullig,
Killorglin, Co Kerry
066-9769892

KILTERNAN
Ms. Mary Montaut
4 Mount Pleasant Villas
Bray, Co. Wicklow
01 2860497

MID KILKENNY,
Mr John Ryan
Kiltown, Castlecomer,
Co Kilkenny.
056-4441375

NEW ROSS,
Mr Seamus Kennedy
Churchtown, Fethard-on-Sea,
New Ross, Co. Wexford
051 397259

NORTH CORK, Mr Moss Guiry
Belview, Bruree, Co Limerick
061-397040

NORTH KILDARE, Mr Sean Byrne
53 Moorfielf Park,
Newbridge, Co. Kildare
045 432048

NORTH MONAHGAN
Mrs Joanna McGlaughlin
35 CastleLane,
Caledon,
Co. Tyrone, BT68 4UB
048 37569548

NORTH TIPPERARY,
Mr. Jim Ryan
"Innisfail" Kirkham St
Thurles, Co. Tipperary
0504 22228

ROUNDWOOD, Mrs M O'Byrne
Carrig View, Moneystown
South, Roundwood,
Wicklow 0404 45209

S. KILDARE,
Mr Mike Cummins
Garretfield, Donard,
Co Wicklow.
087-2726177

S. KILKENNY,
Mr Richard Moran
Kilbline, Bennetsbridge,
Co Kilkenny.
056-7727457

S. TIPPERARY, Mr Tom Prendergast
Ballypatrick, Clonmel,
Co Tipperary
087 9109360

S. WEST CORK,Mr John Bryan
Currarane,Kilbrittan,
Co Cork, 023 49625

S. WEXFORD,Mr James Hogan
Castlebridge,
Co Wexford,
053 9159202

SUCK VALLEY, Mr Frank Kenny
Stonepark, Roscommon
0906 626156

THE KINGDOM, Mr Jim Clerkin,
Arabella House
Ballymacelligott,Tralee
Co Kerry,
066 7137611

THE MIDLAND BEEKEEPERS
Mr Jim Donohoe
11 New Ballinderry, Mullingar,
Co Westmeath
044-9340771/086-2555729

THE ROYAL CO
Mrs Martina Keegan
Grange, Bective, Navan,
Co Meath, 046 9029216

WEST CORK
Mr Donald Hanley
Bawnard, Eyeries,
Co Cork,
027 74187

INTERNATIONAL BEE RESEARCH
ASSOCIATION WEB http://www.ibra.org.uk

IBRA - International Bee Research Association promotes the value of bees by providing information on bee science and beekeeping. This charity was founded in 1949 and is supported by members from around the world. IBRA owns one of the largest international collections of bee books and journals, as well as the Eva Crane / IBRA historical collection and a photographic collection. It operates an online bookshop, publishes its own books and information leaflets, as well as scientific journals.

CORRESPONDENCE TO:
EXECUTIVE DIRECTOR,
Sarah Jones
SCIENTIFIC DIRECTOR,
Norman Carreck

16 North Road,
Cardiff,
CF10 3DY
Tel: 029 2037 2409
Fax: 056 0113 5640
Email: mail@ibra.org.uk

PUBLICATIONS
Journal of Apicultural Research
A peer reviewed scientific journal that's worldwide and world class. This quarterly publication contains the latest high quality original research from around the world, covering aspects of biology, ecology, natural history and culture of all types of bees.

Bee World
The flagship publication for IBRA members. Back after a 4 year hiatus this international journal provides a world view on bees and beekeeping. It covers all topics from bee history to the latest finding in bee science.

Journal of ApiProduct and ApiMedical Science
The latest online publication from IBRA launched in 2009. This peer reviewed journal is dedicated to publishing the latest scientific research on the therapeutic properties of hive products. For more information: www.jaas.org.uk

IBRA

✉ ☎

IBRA BOOKSHOP
The bookshop is accessible via the web site. To support our charitable status IBRA
sells a wide range of publications at competitive prices as well as posters, gifts,
DVD's and sundries. IBRA is also a publishing house and offers its members a
reduction on IBRA products.

MEMBERSHIP
IBRA is proud of its international status and this is reflected by its members who join
from all over the world. The membership package now offers more value than ever
before: quarterly issues of Bee World, a discount on IBRA publications and online
access to a growing back catalogue. For other benefits and the latest information
please visit the web site.

Information about all IBRA publications and services can be found via our web site:
www.ibra.org.uk

INIB
⊠ ☎

THE INSTITUTE OF NORTHERN IRELAND BEEKEEPERS (INIB)

www.inibeekeepers.com

James E. Tew, PhD, Alabama Cooperative Extension Service, State Beekeeping Specialist, Visiting Professor, Auburn University Professor Emeritus, The Ohio State University, will be giving a talk on Saturday 11th February 2012 at The Village Centre, Hillsborough BT26 6AR
Annual Conference and Honey Show, 19th October 2012 (t.b.c.)
The Village Centre, Hillsborough BT26 6AR

Objectives of the Institute
The Institute is established to advance the service of apiculture and to promote and foster the education of the people of Northern Ireland and surrounding environs without distinction of age, gender, disability, sexual orientation, nationality, ethnic identity, political or religious opinion, by associating the statutory authorities, community and voluntary organisations and the inhabitants in a common effort to advance education, and in particular:
a) to raise awareness amongst the beneficiaries about bees, bee-keeping and methods of management;
b) to foster an atmosphere of mutual support among bee-keepers and to encourage the sharing of information and provision of helpful assistance amongst each other.

Affiliation
INIB is affiliated to the British Beekeepers Association.
With 21,100 members the British Beekeepers Association (BBKA) is the leading organisation representing beekeepers within the UK.
As an INIB member, affiliation gives the following benefits.
• BBKA News
• Public Liability Insurance
• Product Liability Insurance
• Bee Disease Insurance available
• Free Information Leaflets to Download
• Members Password Protected Area and Discussion Forum
• Correspondence Courses
• Examination and Assessment Programme
• Telephone Information
• Research Support
• Legal advice
• Representation and lobbying of Government, EU and official bodies.

Clogher Valley Beekeepers Association is affiliated to INIB
Email: cloghervalley@onlineni.net

INIB
✉ ☎

Events
The Institute holds an annual conference and honey show.
The Institute brings to Northern Ireland world renowned expert
speakers from USA and Europe to give talks to beekeepers on
the latest research and up to date beekeeping methods.

Education
Demonstrations on various topics such as mead making,
preparing honey for shows are held during the year.
Courses for honey judges are available.

Honey Bees On Line Studies
INIB has a strong relationship with Professor Jurgen Tautz's of
BEEgrouup Biozentrum Universitaet Wuerzburg and his Honey
Bee On Line Studies project which continues to develop.

MEMBERSHIP SECRETARY
Lyndon Wortley
Teemore Grange
224 Marlacoo Rd,
Portadown,
BT62 3TD
02838841287
eawortley@aol.com

CHAIRMAN
Michael Young MBE
101 Carnreagh,
Hillsborough
BT26 6LJ
02892689724
secretary@
inibeekeepers.com

Holders of the Institute of Northern Ireland Beekeepers Honey Judge Certificate

No.	Name	Phone	Email
001.	MICHAEL BADGER MBE	01132 945879	BUZZ.BUZZ@NTLWORLD.COM
002.	GAIL ORR	02892 638363	GAIL.ORR@BELFASTTRUST.HSCNI.NET
003.	CECIL MCMULLAN	02892 638675	MADELINE.MCMULLAN@HOTMAIL.CO.UK
004.	HUGH MCBRIDE	02825 640872	LORRAINE.MCBRIDE@CARE4FREE.NET
005.	LORRAINE MC BRIDE	02825 640872	LORRAINE.MCBRIDE@CARE4FREE.NET
006.	BILLY DOUGLAS	02897 562926	
007.	MICHAEL YOUNG MBE	02892 689724	MYOUNGJUDGE@YAHOO.CO.UK
008.	FRANCIS CAPENER	01303 254579	FRANCIS@HONEYSHOW.FREESERVE.CO.UK
009.	MARGARET DAVIES	01202 526077	MARG@JDAVIES.FREESERVE.CO.UK
010.	IAN CRAIG	01505 322684	IAN'AT'IANCRAIG.WANADOO.CO.UK
011.	DINAH SWEET	02920 756483	
012.	HENRY J FERGUSON	01550 777132	
013.	LESLIE M WEBSTER	01466 771351	LESWEBSTER@MICROGRAM.CO.UK
014.	REDMOND WILLIAMS	003535242617	EMWILLIAMS@EIRCOM.NET
015.	TERRY ASHLEY	01270 760757	TERRY.ASHLEY@FERA.GSI.GOV.UK
016.	IVOR FLATMAN	01924 257089	IVORFLATMAN@SUPANET.COM
017.	ALAN WOODWARD	01302 868169	JANET.WOODWARD@VIRGIN.NET
018.	DENNIS ATKINSON	01995 602058	DHMATKINSON@TESCO.NET
019	LEO MCGUINNESS	028711 811043	PMCGUINNESS@GLENDERMOTT.COM
020	TOM CANNING	02838 871260	TOM.CANNING@VIRGIN.NET

USA
019. ROBERT BREWER   RBREWER@ARCHES.UGA.EDU
020. ANN HARMAN   AHWORKERB@AOL.COM
021. BOB COLE

LASI
✉ ☎

LABRATORY OF APICULTURE & SOCIAL INSECTS (LASI)

UNIVERSITY OF SUSSEX

FURTHER INFORMATION CONTACT
PDr. Francis L. W. Ratnieks,
Professor of Apiculture
Laboratory of Apiculture &
Social Insects (LASI)
Department of Biological &
Environmental Science
University of Sussex, Falmer,
Brighton BN1 9QG, UK

tel: 01273 872954 (landline),
07766270434 (mob)
F.Ratnieks@Sussex.ac.uk

LASI was founded in 1995 and is headed by Dr. Francis Ratnieks, who is the UK's only Professor of Apiculture. Professor Ratnieks received his training in honey bee biology in the USA at Cornell University and at the University of California. Also in the USA, he was a part-time commercial beekeeper with up to 180 hives used for almond pollination and comb honey production. From 1995 to 2007 LASI was based at the University of Sheffield. In February 2008 Professor Ratnieks moved to the University of Sussex. Sussex University has provided a new laboratory that is ideal for honey bee research. There is a large adjoining apiary with an equipment shed and workshop, and the laboratory is only 100m from the main biology building. There are further apiaries on the university campus just 5 minutes walk away.

LASI is the largest university-based laboratory studying honey bees in the UK and is set up both to do research on honey bee biology and to train the next generation of honey bee scientists. Undergraduate students can do research projects on honey bee biology in their final year, and also receive lectures on honey bee biology. Graduate students can take a PhD in a particular area of honey bee biology. Postdoctoral researchers study honey bees and learn new skills to complement the training they received while doing their PhD.

LASI research focuses on both basic and applied questions in honey bee biology and beekeeping. Research areas include: how honey bees organize their colonies, how they resolve their conflicts, nestmate recognition and guarding, foraging, mating, improved beekeeping techniques, bee health and breeding, conservation of native honey bees.

LASI's mission is to be an international centre of research excellence, to train the next generation of bee researchers, and to be a resource for UK beekeepers and the public in general.

NAT MAGS

(INTER/) NATIONAL PERIODICALS

AMERICAN BEE JOURNAL
(US monthly)
Agents: Northern Bee Books
Scout Bottom Farm,
Mytholmroyd,HX7 5JS
& E.H. Thorne Ltd
Beehive Works Wragby
LN3 5LA
AUSTRALASIAN BEEKEEPER
(Monthly).
Subscriptions US$38
Sample from: Penders PMB
19 Maitland, NSW 2320
Australia
BEE CRAFT
Official monthly journal
of the British Beekeepers
Association
Subscriptions and enquiries to:
Sue Jakeman
Bee Craft Ltd
107 Church St,
Werrington
Peterborough
PE4 6QF
secretary@bee-craft.com
www.bee-craft.com
01733 771221
BEEKEEPERS QUARTERLY, THE
Companion to the
Beekeepers Annual
Subscriptions £26 p.a (but
group schemes at reduced

rates exist for BKAs)
from: Northern Bee Books
Scout Bottom Farm
Mytholmroyd, Hebden
Bridge, W. Yorkshire HX7 5JS
**BERKSHIRE BEEKEEPERS
ASSOCIATIONS, FEDERATION OF
(FBBKA)**
Newsletter Editor,
Mr R F Crocker
25 Shiplake Bottom
Peppard Common
Oxon RG9 5HH
0118 9722315
berksbees@btopenworld.
com
CHESHIRE BEEKEEPER
The Newsletter of CBKA
Mr P Sutcliffe
2 Hatfield Court,
Holmes Chapel
Cheshire CW4 7HP
h.p.sutcliffe@googlemail.
com
GLEANINGS IN BEE CULTURE
US monthly
From: Northern Bee Books
Scout Bottom Farm,
Mytholmroyd,HX7 5JS
& E.H. Thorne Ltd
Beehive Works Wragby
LN3 5LA

**INDIAN BEE JOURNAL IN
ENGLISH**
1325 Sadashiv Peth, Poona
411 8030, India
**INTERNATIONAL BEE RESEARCH
ASSOCIATION**
Journal of Apicultural Research
Journal of ApiProduct and
ApiMedical Science
Bee World
enquires to:
16 North Road
Cardiff
CF10 3DY
mail@ibra.org.uk
IRISH BEEKEEPER
(Monthly) Editor: Jim Ryan
Inisfail, Kickham Street
Thurles, Co. Tipperary
jimbee1@eircom.net
**THE NEW ZEALAND
BEEKEEPER JOURNAL**
Published 11 issues per year
for National BKA of
New Zealand
Contact: Jessica Williams
Executive Secretary
National Beekeepers
Association
PO Box 10792
Wellington 6143
New Zealand

NAT MAGS

✉ ☎

P: + 64 4 471 6254
F: + 64 4 499 0876
Tsecretary@nba.org.nz

BEEKEEPER, THE Magazine
of the Scottish BKA.
Membership terms **from:**
Enid Brown, Milton House,
Main Street, Scotlandwell
Kinross-shire KY13 9JA
Sample copy to view online
www.scottishbeekeepers.
org.uk

SOUTH AFRICAN BEE JOURNAL
Bi-monthly. P.O. Box 41
Modderfontein, 1645, RSA.
THE SPEEDY BEE
Monthly US newspaper,
£24 **from:** NBB,
Scout Bottom Farm,
Mytholmroyd
Hebden Bridge HX7 5JS

**GWENYNWYR CYMRU /
WELSH BEEKEEPER,
EDITOR, Duncan Parks**
Cefn Coed
Graianrmon yn Ial
Mold CH7 4QW
01824 780504
fax 01824 780822
e-mail,
Duncan@The-Parks.com
The publication of the Welsh
Beekeepers Association
giving news and views of
beekeeping in Wales
and abroad.

Golygydd/Editor: A Duncan
Parks, Cefn Coed, Ffordd
Graianrhyd, Llanarmon yn Ial
YR WYDDGRUG CH7 4QW
(01824) 780 504
e-mail,
duncan@the-parks.com
Erthyglau Cymraeg: Dewi
Morris Jones, Llwynderw
Bronant
Aberystwyth SY23 4TG
Manylion tanysgrifau/
Subscription Details:
H. I. Morris, Golygfan
Llangynin, Sancler
CAERFYRDDIN SA33 4JZ
01944 290885

THE NATIONAL DIPLOMA IN BEEKEEPING

HON. SECRETARY
Mrs Margaret Thomas
Tig na Bruaich,
Taybridge Terrace,
Aberfeldy, Perthshire,
PH15 2BS.

CHAIRMAN, Dr David Aston NDB
38 Wressle, Selby
YO8 6ET
01757 638758

The Examinations B oard for the National Diploma in Beekeeping was set up in 1954 to meet a need for a beekeeping qualification above the level of the highest certificate awarded by the British, Scottish, Welsh and Ulster Associations.

The Diploma Examination, as designed by the Board, was considered to be an appropriate qualification for a County Beekeeping Lecturer or a specialist appointment requiring a high level of academic and practical ability in beekeeping. It is the highest beekeeping qualification recognised in the British Isles and a high percentage of the past and present holders of the Diploma have given distinguished service to beekeeping education at all levels.

Although the post of County Beekeeping Lecturer has now disappeared, this has merely emphasised the need for some beekeepers to face the challenge of this examination and maintain the high level skills and knowledge needed to keep pace with the increased problems facing all beekeepers at the present time.

The Board consists of representatives from a wide range of organisations and from Government Departments and together form an impressive amalgam of expert knowledge in Beekeeping and Education. Although the National Beekeeping Associations are represented on the Board it is entirely independent of them.

Normally the highest certificate of one of the National Associations is a necessary criterion for eligibility to take the Examination for the Diploma which is held in alternate years. The Written Examination is taken in March, and the Practical, in three sections plus a viva-voce is held in June.

The Board also organises an annual Advanced Beekeeping Course covering various parts of the syllabus that are difficult to cover by independent study. Lasting

NDB

a working week, they cover the main sections of the Syllabus and represent the highest level of training available to British Beekeepers at the present time. The outside lecturers are each acknowledged experts in their particular field. In recent years the Board have been privileged to hold their course at the Fera National Bee Unit at Sand Hutton, York.

For further details regarding the Diploma write, enclosing a stamped A4 SAE to the Secretary, or visit our website: http://www.national-diploma-bees.org.uk/

Those who have gained the National Diploma in Beekeeping

Matthew Allan	Celia Davis	Geoff Ingold	Fred Richards
Harry Allen	Ivor Davis	George Jenner	E. Roberts
Harrison Ashforth	Alec S.C. Deans	C. F. Jesson	Arthur Rolt
John Ashton	Clive de Bruyn	A.C. Kessel	Jeff Rounce
Dianne Askquith-Ellis	A.P. Draycott	W.E. Large	Graham Royle
David Aston	M. Feeley	G.W. Lumsden	J. Ryding
John Atkinson	Barry Fletcher	Henry Luxton	J.H. Savage
Miss E.E. Avey	David Frimston	A.S. McClymont	Donald Sims
Ken Basterfield	Oonagh Gabriel	J.L. MacGregor	F.G. Smith
Bridget Beattie	George Gill	Ian McLean	George Smith
Brig. H.T. Bell	Reg Gove	Ian A. Maxwell	J.H.F. Smith
R.W. Brooke	Eric Greenwood	Paul Metcalf	Robert Smith
Norman Carreck	Pam Gregory	J. Mills	Ken Stevens
Rosina Clark	Anthony R.W. Griffin	Bernhard Mobus	J. Swarbrick
Charles Collins	Robert Hammond	G. N'tonga	Margaret Thomas
Gerry Collins	Ben Harden	Peter Oldrieve	John Walker
Tom Collins	C.A. Harwood	Gillian Partridge	Adrian Waring
Robert Couston	Leslie Hender	E.H. Pee	Brian Welch
John Cowan	Alf Hebden	L.E. Perera	J. Wilbraham
S. J. Cox	Ted Hooper	E.R. Poole	
Jim Crundwell	Geoff Hopkinson	Bill Reynolds	
Beulah Cullen	G. Howatson	Pat Rich	

THE NATIONAL HONEY SHOW

www.honeyshow.co.uk
THE 2011 SHOW IS AT ST GEORGE'S COLLEGE,
WEYBRIDGE, SURREY KT15 2QS
27TH – 29TH OCTOBER 2011.

This venue is excellent

Just off the M25 junction 11
Rail from Waterloo to Weybridge or Addlestone

Free car parking

The Show itself is a wonderful competitive exhibition
of all the products of the bee-hive, coupled with an
excellent series of lectures, workshops and a wide
variety of trade and educational stands.

We recommend that you attend all three days, and
suggest that you become a member of the Show –
just **£10.00** per annum

For further information, please write to the Hon General
Secretary, or Email: showsec@zbee.com or visit our
website www.honeyshow.co.uk

HON. GENERAL SECRETARY
REV. H.F CAPENER
1 Baldric Road
Folkestone CT20 2NR

HON TREASURER
C S Mence
27 Acacia Grove
New Malden, Surrey KT3 3BJ

PUT THIS DATE IN YOUR DIARY
27TH – 29TH OCTOBER 2012

THE.NATIONAL

HONEY.SHOW

www.honeyshow.co.uk
THE 2012 SHOW IS
AT ST GEORGE'S COLLEGE,
WEYBRIDGE
27TH - 29TH OCTOBER

RR

✉ ☎

ROTHAMSTED RESEARCH

www.rothamsted.bbsrc.ac.uk

ROTHAMSTED
RESEARCH

ROTHAMSTED RESEARCH
Plant and Invertebrate
Ecology Department
Harpenden
Hertfordshire AL5 2JQ
Tel (01582) 763133
Fax (01582) 760981

**SCIENTISTS INVOLVED IN
BEE RESEARCH
AT ROTHAMSTED**
Dr Juliet Osborne
Dr Jason Lim
Dr Alison Haughton
Dr Stephan Wolf
Dr Matthias Becker
Jennifer Swain
Dr Peter Kennedy
Andrew Martin
Dr Judith Pell
Daniel Basterfield
Simon Jones
Emma Wright
(PhD student)
Peter Tomkins
(beekeeping support).

Rothamsted Research in Harpenden, Hertfordshire, was established in 1843 and is the world's oldest agricultural research station. There has been work on bees continuously since 1923, and despite some funding cuts and the loss of key personnel in recent years, work on bees and pollination continues as a major area of interest. We have ten scientists and students working on bee and pollination projects. A new laboratory for studying bee ecology and behaviour has been built on the Rothamsted farm, and we maintain approximately 40 colonies of honeybees in four apiaries, with help from an experienced beekeeper who was also a previous member of staff.

We study the ecology of insect pollinators and pollen movement between plants, focussing particularly on bumblebees and honeybees. By answering fundamental questions about how bees move around at the landscape scale we hope to be able to make and test predictions about how they transport pollen around, and the consequent effects on bee-mediated plant gene flow. Our team has the overarching aims of 1) conserving and promoting bee populations and 2) protecting and promoting wild flower and crop pollination. We work primarily, but not exclusively, in arable landscapes examining pollination of plant species such as oilseed rape, white clover and borage.

EXAMINING INSECT FLIGHT PATTERNS WITH HARMONIC RADAR
Studying insect flight at a landscape scale requires sophisticated techniques. At Rothamsted we are fortunate to have the only **entomological scanning harmonic**

radar system in the world for tracking individual flying insects. We have used it to track honeybees, bumblebees and butterflies, gaining new insights into their aerial behaviour, as they search for food and fly to and from flower patches. The radar does have its limitations: it can only track insects over about 900m and that is in a relatively flat landscape with low vegetation, but it is very useful for understanding exploratory behaviour in relation to visual and olfactory cues.

HONEYBEE POPULATIONS AND PATHOLOGY

We have a two large projects, jointly funded by BBSRC and Syngenta (in collaboration with Warwick HRI and UFZ Leipzig) and funded by the Insect Pollinator Initiative to examine the effect of multiple stressors on honeybee colony survival. Using a combination of modelling and experiments, we hope to tease apart the interactions between the effects of disease within the colony, and the effect of limited foraging sources in the landscape. We also have a PhD student studying the effects of pathogens on honeybee learning and foraging behaviour. The learning and foraging efficiency of infected and healthy colonies are being compared, and the possible impact on colony survival is then explored.

BUMBLEBEE POPULATIONS AND CONSERVATION

Bumblebees are important in agricultural systems as pollinators of crops and wild flowers, but their numbers and diversity have declined over the last 40 years, particularly in areas of intensively managed agriculture. In agricultural landscapes, the viability of bumblebee colonies depends on both the amount and spatial distribution of forage, in addition to the availability of suitable nesting sites. We use a combination of modelling, field survey, field experimentation and genetics to predict the distribution of bumblebees in arable landscapes, model their long-term viability, and to determine the impacts of change in agricultural regimes.

POLLINATION OF CROPS AND WILD FLOWERS AT THE LANDSCAPE SCALE

We study both the overall level of pollination in crops and wild plants in arable farmland, and also the extent of gene flow between crops or plants. We have shown that seed and fruit set in hedgerow plants can be limited by the availability of pollinators (Jacobs et al 2009). Since this affects berry production it can have a knock-on effect on the number of birds feeding on the hedges in the winter. As part of a BBSRC project (led by University of Stirling), we are examining whether wild plant pollination is influenced by the vicinity of mass-flowering crops such as oilseed rape or field beans and have also compared the pollination of these wild plants in suburban gardens versus arable farmland, showing that the plants get better pollinated in gardens and suggesting that these areas provide good resources to promote the bee populations (Cussans et al 2010).

FUNDING

Rothamsted Research receives funds for research from the BBSRC (Biotechnology and Biological Sciences Research Council of the UK), and we have also been awarded grants from the Insect Pollinator Initiative, from Defra (Dept of Environment, Food and Rural Affairs), the European Union and commercial organisations such as Syngenta. Our research programme has also received generous support from beekeepers via the CB Dennis Fund, from local beekeeping associations and from the BBKA and we are very grateful for this.

For more information visit
http://www.rothamsted.bbsrc.ac.uk

THE SCOTTISH BEEKEEPERS' ASSOCIATION

SBA

AIMS OF THE ASSOCIATION
- publish a monthly magazine
- maintain the Moir Library in Edinburgh
- conduct examinations in the art of beekeeping
- provide insurance and a compensation scheme for members

EDUCATION
The SBA arranges courses and awards certificates to successful candidates in the Scottish Basic Beemaster, Expert Beemaster, Honey Judge and Microscopy Examinations. It also actively promotes beekeeping by informing the public, especially the young, about bees and their benefits to the environment.

INSURANCE AND THE COMPENSATION SCHEME
All members of the SBA have insurance against Public Liability. The SBA Compensation Scheme is restricted to bee colonies located in Scotland and allocates part-replacement value for damage by vandalism, fire, theft and certain brood diseases.

LIBRARY
The SBA Moir Library in Edinburgh has one of the world's finest collection of beekeeping books. A library card is issued annually to every member who can borrow books at the cost of return postage only. Details may be obtained from the Library Convener.

MARKETS
Advice is given on all aspects of marketing honey products at appropriate times. Suggested bulk, wholesale and retail prices are notified in the magazine.

GENERAL SECRETARY
Mrs. Bronwen Wright
20 Lennox Road
Edinburgh EH5 3JW
(0131) 552 3439
e-mail, secretary@
scottishbeekeepers.org.uk

HON PRESIDENT
The Rt. Hon. Earl of Mansfield D.L, J.P
Scone Palace
Perth PH2 6BE

HON. VICE PRES,
Iain F Steven
4 Craigie View
Perth
PH2 0DP
01738 621100

HON. LIBRARIAN
Mrs. Margaret M. Sharp
City Librarian, City Library
George IV Bridge, Edinburgh

HON. LEGAL ADVISER,
Taggert, Meil & Mathers
20 Bon Accord Sq,
Aberdeen
(01224) 588020

159

SBA

HON. AUDITOR, G. Hendry CA
20 Parkhill Crescent,
Dyce Aberdeen
(01224) 724247

PUBLICATIONS

- The Scottish Beekeeper is published monthly and sent post free as part of the annual membership fee of £30 payable to the Membership Convener.
- Introduction to Bees and Beekeeping is £6.00 plus postage and may be obtained from the Advertising and Publicity Convener.

PUBLICITY

Members can purchase the Association tie, lapel badge, car sticker etc. Details may be obtained from the Advertising and Publicity Convener.

SHOWS

Three major annual honey shows are held in Scotland. They are at the Royal Highland Show, Ingliston, Edinburgh in June, while the Scottish National Honey Show and the East of Scotland Honey Show are both held at the Dundee Flower and Food Festival in September. Shows are also held at Aberdeen, Ayr, Inverness and there are 2 shows in Fife.

Executive Committee

PRESIDENT,
Phil McAnespie
12 Monument Road
Ayr KA7 2RL
01292 885660
membership@
scottishbeekeepers.org.uk

VICE PRESIDENT,
Mrs. Bronwen Wright
20 Lennox Road,
Edinburgh EH5 3JW
0131 552 3439
secretary@
scottishbeekeepers.org.uk

IMM. PAST PRES, Alan Teale
8 Mayfield Road
Inverness IV2 4AE
01463 226411
teale@fs.com

Ian Craig
30 Burnside Avenue
Brookfield, Johnstone
Renfrewshire PA5 8UT
01505 322684
ian@iancraig.
wanadoo.co.uk

GENERAL SEC
Mrs. Bronwen Wright
20 Lennox Road,
Edinburgh EH5 3JW
0131 552 3439
secretary@
scottishbeekeepers.org.uk

SBA CO-ORDINATOR,
Iain F. Steven
4 Craigie View, Perth PH2 0DP
01738 621100
lomand@btinternet.com

TREASURER, Mrs. Barbara Cruden
Standing Stones, Dyce
Aberdeen AB21 0HH
01224 770001
barbara.cruden@btinternet.
com

EDITOR, SCOTTISH BEEKEEPER,
Nigel Southworth
47 Middleton Road, Uphall,
Edinburgh, EH52 5DF
01506 865762
editorscottishbeekeeper@
gmail.com

CONVENERS OF STANDING COMMITTEES

MEMBERSHIP CONVENER
P. McAnespie
12 Monument Rd.Ayr
KA7 2RL   01292 885660
membership@
scottishbeekeepers.org.uk
INSURANCE & COMPENSATION
C. Irwin
55 Lindsaybeg Rd
Chryston, Glasgow
G69 9DW
0141 7791333
ceirwin@talktalk.net
ADVERTISING & PUBLICITY
Miss E Brown
Milton House, Main Street
Scotlandwell, Kinross
KY13 9JA   01592 840582
honeybees@onetel.com
EDUCATION, Ian Craig
30 Burnside Avenue
Brookfield. Johnstone
Renfrewshire PA5 8UT
01505 322684
ian@iancraig.wanadoo.
co.uk

SHOWS, Miss E Brown
Milton House, Main Street
Scotlandwell, Kinross
KY13 9JA
01592 840582
honeybees@onetel.com
LIBRARY, Mrs Una Robertson
13 Wardie Ave
Edinburgh
EH5 2AB
una.robertson@btinternet.
com
MARKETS, John Durkacz
15 Lundin Road
Crossford
Fife KY12 8PW
01383 722186
Durkacz@hotmail.co.uk
BEE DISEASES, Phil Moss
Ealachan Bhana
Clachan Seil
Oban
PA34 4TL
01852 300383
phil.moss@dsl.pipex.com

AREA REPRESENTATIVES
NORTH,
Mrs Sheila Barnard
Viewmount, Tobermory,
Isle of Mull
PA75 6PG
01688 302008
tim-barnard@lineone.net
EAST, John Trout
13 Middlebank Holdings
Dunfirmline, Fife
KY11 8QN
01383 415534
dwf@fifebeekeepers.co.uk
WEST, Peter Stromberg
21 Woodside
Houston, Renfrewshire
PA6 7DD
01505 613830
pstromberg1@aol.com
ABERDEEN, Mrs. Hazel MacKenzie
Invercraig, Kingswell
Aberdeen
AB15 8PT
01224 740837
hazelmackenzie900@
btinternet/com

OFFICERS

PROMOTION OF BEEKEEPING,
P Mathews Mrs C Mathews
4 Annanhill
Annan
Dumfries-shire
DG12 6TN
01461 205525
silverhive@hotmail.com

WEBMASTER, Alisdair Joyce
Manachie Lodge.
Dallas Dhu
Forres
IV36 0RR
01309 671288
webmaster@
scottishbeekeepers.org.uk

SBA

✉ ☎

S.B.A LECTURERS *Addresses in SBA Honey Judges List

All those listed claim expenses (except G. Sharpe, Bees adviser funded by SGRPID),
All speakers accompany talks with visual aids

* MISS. E. BROWN (General)
01592 840542
* M BADGER (General)
0113 2945879
* I. CRAIG (General)
01505 322684
A.B. FERGUSON
(General, Varroa)
Firparkneuk. Kirtlebridge
Lockerbie   DG11 3LZ
01461 500322
* C. IRWIN (General)
0141 7791333
* DR. F. ISLES (Bee diseases)
01382 370 315
M.M. PETERSON
(Bee genetics)
Balhaldie House,
High street, Dunblane
FK15 0ER
01786 822093

MRS. U. A. ROBERTSON
(History of SBA, Moir Library,
History of beekeeping)
13 Wardie Ave
Edinburgh EH5 2AB
0131 552 5341
G. SHARPE (SAC) (Varroa
Management: My apiary
management system)
Apiculture Specialist
Life Science Technology
Group, SAC Auchincruive
Ayr KA6 5HW
01292 525375
Mrs M Thomas (General)
Tighnabraich, Taybridge
Terrace, Aberfeldy
Perthshire PH15 2BS
01887 829710

J. TYLER (Strain selection
and queen breeding)
22 Montgomerie Drive
Fairlie, Ayrshire
01475 568421
* L. M. WEBSTER (General)
01466 771351
DR G RAMSAY (Beekeeping on
the Internet / Can Bees fight
Varroa?)
Parkview, Station Road
Errol, Perth   PH2 7SN
01821 642385
A RIACH
(Beehives through the Ages)
Woodgate, 7 Newland Ave
Bathgate
EH48 1EE
01506 653839

MEMBER ASSOCIATIONS AND THEIR SECRETARIES

ABERDEEN, Rosie Crighton
29 Marcus Cresc
Blackburn, Aberdeen
AB21 0SZ
01224 791181
rosie@crighton-finflater.
fsbusuness.co.uk
AYR, Mrs L Baillie
Windyhill Cottage
Uplands Rd, Sundrum
Ayre, KA6 5JU
01292 570659
BORDER, Norman Jarvis
6 Dean Road, Sprouston,
Kelso TD5 8HN
01573 228276
noel.tweedview@
btopenworld.com

CADDONFOOT,
James & Julia Edey
West Water, Bedrule, Hawick,
Roxburghshire,
TD9 8TD
01450 870400
jamesedey@googlemail.com
CLYDE AREA, Mr George Morrison
102 Woodside Ave Bearsden
G61 2NZ
0141 942 9419
COWAL, Brian Madden
123a Alexandra Parade
Dunoon,
PA23 8AW
01369 703317

DINGWALL
Ms Sarah Smythe
14 Cromarty Drive
Strathpeffer
Ross and Cromarty
IV14 9DB
01997 420000
dingwall.beekeeping@
googlemail.com
DUNBLANE & STIRLING,
Fiona Fernie
Greystones
Dunira, By Comtie
PH6 2JZ
01764 679152
secretary@dsbka.net

DUNFERMLINE & WEST FIFE
Dr T Scott
Grange Farmhouse
Grange Rd, Dunfermline
KY11 3DG
01383 733125
dwf@fifebeekeepers.co.uk

EAST OF SCOTLAND
Mrs Susan Anderson
12 Kirkgate, Letham,
Forfar DD8 2XQ
01307 819477
anderson44 @talktalk.net

EAST LOTHIAN, Mrs Jo Dodds
20 Kings Avenue
Longniddry, East Lothian
EH32 0QN
01875 852916
eastlothianbeekeepers@
gmail.com

EASTER ROSS
Mrs P Douglas-Menzies
Cardboll Cottage, Fearn
Ross-shire, IV20 1XP
01862 871572

EASTWOOD, Graham Matuszak
Flat1/2, 29 Herriot Street
Pollockshields
Glasgow G41 2NN
0141 418 0449
grahammatuszak@hotmail.
com

EDINBURGH & MIDLOTHIAN
P Steven
Eastercowden Cottage
Dalkeith, Midlothian
EH22 2NS
07703 528801

FIFE, Janice Furness
The Dirdale, Boarhills
St. Andrews, Fife KY16 8PP
01334 880 469
jcfurness@dirdale.fsnet.co.uk

FORTINGALL, Mrs. Jo Pendleton,
Lilac Cottage
Old Bridge of Tilt
by Pitlochry
PH18 5TP
01796 481 362

GLASGOW DISTRICT,
Mr P Stromberg
21 Woodside Houston,
Renfrewshire
PA6 7DD
01505 613830

HELENSBURGH, M Thornley
Glenarn, Glenarn Road
Rhu, Helensburgh
G84 8LL
01436 820493
masthome@dsl.pipex.com

INVERNESS-SHIRE
Mrs S Forth
Kirkland Lodge
Wardlaw Road
Kirkhill, Inverness-shire
IV5 7NB
01463 831511

KELVIN VALLEY, I Ferguson
4 South Glassford Street
Milngavie G62 6AT
0141 956 3963

KILBARCHAN AND DISTRICT
I. Craig
30 Burnside Ave
Brookfield
Johnstone PA5 8UT
01505 322684

KILMARNOCK & IRVINE
J. Campbell
North Kilbryde House
Stewarton
Kilmarnock KA3 3EP
01560 482489

KIRRIEMUIR,
'Disbanded'

LARGS & DIST, Kate Dahlstrom
3 Burnside Road
Largs KA30 9BY
01475 740437
k.dahlstrom@btinternet.com

LOCHABER, Rev Kate Atchley
Anasmara, Mingarry
Acharacle, Inverness-shire
PH36 4JX
01967 431420
contact@kateatchley.co.uk

MORAY, T Harris
Cowiemuir, Fochabers
01343 821 282

MULL, Mrs. S. Barnard
Viewmount, Tobermory
Isle of Mull PA75 6PG
01688 302008

NAIRN & DISTRICT, John Burns
Woodlands, Cawdor Road
Nairn IV12 5EF
01667 454887
jandjburns@hotmail.com

OBAN & DISTRICT,
Phil Moss
Ealachan Bhana
Clachan Seil
Oban PA34 4TL
01852 300383
phil.moss@dsl.pipex.com

OLRIG and District, Robin Inglis
Roadside Skirza
Freswick, Wick KW1 4XX
01955 611260
gailinglis@btinternet.com

ORKNEY, Doris Fischler
84 Victoria street
Stromness
Orkney KW16 3BS
01856 850447
d@orcahotel.com

SBA

✉ ☎

PEEBLES-SHIRE,
Amanda Clydesdale
20 Kingsmeadows Gardens
Peebles EH45 9LB
01721 720563
amanda.clydesdale@
btinternet.com
PERTHSHIRE, J. Shovlin
"Invercarse", 4 Glebe
Terrace, Perth PH2 7AG
01738 627965
SKYE & LOCHALSH, M Purrett
15 Glasnakille, Egol
Isle of Skye, IV49 9BQ
01471 866 207
S. OF SCOTLAND, A Ferguson
Firparkneuk
Kirtlebridge Lockerbie
DG11 3LZ   01461 500322
fergiearchie@tiscali.co.uk
SUTHERLAND, Sue Steven
Mulberry Croft, 2 East
Newport, Berriedale
Caithness KW7 6HA
01539 751 245
WEST'N GALLOWAY, Fiona Keith
The Walled Garden
Dunragit DG9 8PH
01581 400613
WEST LINTON & DISTRICT
D. Stokes
100 Main Street, Roslin
Midlothian EH25 9LT
0131 440 3477

M BADGER
Kara, 14 Thorn Lane,
Roundhay,
Leeds LS8 1NN
MISS E. BROWN
Milton House, Main Street,
Scotlandwell
Kinross KY13 9JA
01592 840582
P.J. BROWNE
The Rowan Tree, Gairlochy
Spean Bridge
Inverness-shire PH34 4EQ
01397 712730
M. CANHAM
Whinhill Farm House
by Cawdor, Nairn IV12 5RF
01667 404314
I. CRAIG
30 Burnside Avenue
Brookfield, Johnstone
Renfrewshire,PA5 8UT
01505 322684
H DONOHOE
7 Grant Road
Banchory AB31 5UW
01330 823502
C. E. IRWIN
55 Lindsaybeg Road
Chryston, Glasgow
G69 9DW
0141 7791333
DR F. ISLES
"Gardenhurst",
Newbigging Broughty Ferry
Dundee DD5 3RH
01382 370315

P MATHEWS
MRS C MATHEWS
4 Annanhill
Annan, Dumfries-shire
DG12 6TN
01461 205525
MS B L MCLEAN
Upper Flat, 2 Invererne Rd,
Forres IV36 1DZ
01309 676316
W.B. TAYLOR
West Newbigging Cottage,
Glenbervie Road, Drumlithie
Stonehaven AB39 3YA
01569 740375
L.M. WEBSTER
Birchlea, Rothiemay, Huntly
Aberdeenshire AB54 5LN
01466 771351
C. WEIGHTMAN
Shilford, Stocksfield,
Northumberland NE43 4HW
01661 842082
C. WILSON
Cedarhill, Auchencloch,
Banknock, Bonnybridge
FK4 1VA
01324 840227
DR D WRIGHT
MRS B WRIGHT
20 Lennox Row
Edinburgh EH3 5JW
0131 552 3439
M. YOUNG
101 Carnreagh, Hillsborough
County Down
N. Ireland BT26 6LJ
0289 268972

Freuchie BKA disbanded

ULSTER BEEKEEPERS' ASSOCIATION

UBKA

www.ubka.org

OBJECTS OF THE ASSOCIATION

The objects of the Association are to unite beekeepers for their mutual benefit to serve the best interests of beekeeping by all means within its power and to foster its healthy development.

For the purpose of achieving these objects the Association will:

- promote the formation of local Beekeepers' Associations
- disseminate information and advice about beekeeping
- provide examination facilities in the art of beekeeping
- encourage maintainenance and improvement of the beekeeping environment.

EDUCATION

In conjunction with the College of Agriculture, Food & Enterprise (CAFRE), the U.B.K.A. assists in organising classes for Preliminary, Intermediate and Senior Certificate Examinations in Beekeeping following the syllabus of the F.I.B.K.A.

INSURANCE

Affiliated local Associations and their individual members have access to the UBKA group public and product liability insurance scheme.

APIARY SITES

The ten local Associations and CAFRE's Greenmount Campus have access to apiary sites and, for some sites, access to observation houses, provided with help affiliated local Associations and CAFRE's Greenmount Campus each have an apiary site with observation houses, provided with help from Leader 2 funding, for use in demonstrating and promoting good practice to members, schools and other interested groups

PRESIDENT,
David Wright
24 Quarry Road
Lisbane, Comber,
Newtownards
Co Down BT23 5NF

CHAIRMAN, John Witchell
40 Hollywood Road,
Newtownards
Co. Down BT23 4TQ

TREASURER, Matthew Porter.
375 Old Glenarm Road
LARNE Co Antrim
BT40 2LH

LECTURERS
Jim Fletcher
26 Coach Road, Comber
Co.Down. BT23 5QX

Ethel Irvine
2 Laragh Lee
Ballycassidy
ENNISKILLEN
BT94 2JT

Lorraine McBride
11, Ballyloughan Park
Ballymena, Co.Antrim,
BT43 5HW

Norman Walsh
43, Edentrillick Rd
Hillsborough, Co. Down
BT26 6PG

UBKA

LECTURERS CONTINUED

Rev Sam Millar
41 Rectory Park
Garvagh, COLERAINE
Co Londonderry BT51 5AJ

HONEY JUDGES
Jim Fletcher
26 Coach Road, Comber
BT23 5QX
Norman Walsh
43 Edentrillick Rd
Hillsborough Co. Down
BT26 6NH
Michael Young
Mileway, Carnreagh Road
Hillsborough, Co. Down
BT26 6LJ

HONEY SHOWS

Local Associations, Horticultural and other Societies stage honey shows throughout Northern Ireland. The Northern Ireland Honey Show hosted by the Belfast City Parks Department is held annually in September in the Botanic Gardens Belfast.

CONFERENCE

The 68th UBKA Annual Conference will be held on 24 – 25 February 2012 at CAFRE's Greenmount Campus, Antrim. Contact the U.B.K.A. Conference Manager at 028 9445 3892 and www.ubka.org for details.

SECRETARIES OF ASSOCIATIONS

BELFAST,
Alan Rea
12 Kirkliston Drive
Belfast BT5 5NX

DROMORE AND DISTRICT,
Patrick Lundy
116 Dromore Road,
Ballynahinch,
Co.Down BT24 8HK

EAST ANTRIM,
Fiona McGinty
1 Berkeley Deane
Greenisland
CARRICKFERGUS
Co Antrim, BT38 8FX

MID ANTRIM,
Lorraine McBride
11 Ballyloughlan Park
BALLYMENA,Co. Antrim
BT43 5HW

FERMANAGH,
Brian Richardson
agho,305 LattoneRoad,
Belcoo, ENNISKILLEN
Co. Ferman

KILLINCHY AND DISTRICT
David McCartney
19 Delacherois Ave, Lisburn,
Co. Antrim BT27 4TR

MID ULSTER, Ernie Watterson
Flourmill Hill,
264 Coalisland Rd
DUNGANNON
Co.Tyrone BT71 6EP

RANDALSTOWN,
Caroline Thomson
105 Cidercourt Rd
Crumlin, ANTRIM,
Co. Antrim, BT29 4RX

ROE VALLEY, Billy McBride
59, Seacoast Road,
Limavady
Co. Londonderry
BT49 9DW

ROSTREVOR AND
WARRENPOINT
Cécile Maugy
5 Killowen Old Road
Rostrevor, County Down
BT34 3AD

CYMDEITHAS GWENYNWYR

CYMRU WELSH BEEKEEPERS' ASSOCIATION

AMCANION Y GYMDEITHAS / AIMS OF THE ASSOCIATION
- Promote and develop beekeeping in Wales
- Conduct examinations in beekeeping
- Liaise with organisations and bodies for the benefit of beekeeping in Wales

AELODAETH UNIGOL / INDIVIDUAL MEMBERSHIP
Individual membership of the WBKA is provided for persons who do not live within the areas of branch associations, and wish to support the association. Information relating to benefits and facilities provided for individual members is available from the Individual Membership Secretary.

ARHOLIADAU / EXAMINATIONS
The Examinations Board conducts six grades of examinations: Junior, Primary, Intermediate, Practical, Honey Show Judges, Senior. Information is available from the Examination Board Secretary.

Candidates following the Duke of Edinburgh Award Scheme may receive information regarding the inclusion of beekeeping as a course submission from the Examinations Secretary.

CYNHADLEDD/ CONVENTION
At the Royal Welsh Agricultural Society's Showground, Llanelwedd. This event is normally held during Late March/ Early April. Information relating to this event is available from the convention secretary.

YSWIRIANT / INSURANCE
All individual and fully paid up members of beekeeping associations affiliated to WBKA are covered against 'Public and Product' liability claims. All affiliated associations are covered against public liability during conventions officially organised by the association.

YSGRIFENNYDD / SECRETARY
Lynfa Davies
Godre'r Coed
Devils Bridge
Aberystwyth SY23 4QY
secretary@wbka.com

LLYWYDD/PRESIDENT
Dinah Sweet,
Graig Fawr Lodge
Caerphilly
CF83 1NF
president@wbka.com

CADEIRYDD/CHAIR
Valerie Forsyth
Bwlch y Rhyd
Nanternis
New Quay
SA45 9RS
chair@wbka.com

IS-GADAIRYDD/
VICE CHAIR
Tom Pegg
depchair@wbka.com

WBKA/CGC

✉ ☎

TRYSORYDD/TREASURER
Jane Jamison
Riverside House
Spring Gardens
St Dogmaels, Cardigan
SA43 3AX
treasurer@wbka.com

The WBKA Individual Membership benefits include cover under the BDI Scheme against the loss, due to foul brood diseases, of a minimum number of stocks (determined by BDI). Affiliated Associations provide this cover for their members.

LLYFRGELL / LIBRARY

The reference sections of all county libraries in Wales have details of the names and addresses of Secretaries of Associations affiliated to WBKA.

Books on beekeeping can be borrowed from county, branch and mobile libraries. The Library, Ffordd y Bala, Dolgellau LL40 2YS, has been nominated to stock beekeeping books.

GWEFEISTR/WEBMASTER
AND GOLYGYDD/EDITOR
Brian and Cherry Clark
editor@wbka.com

Members of associations affiliated to IBRA may borrow books/documents from its library.

GWENYNWYR CYMRU - The Welsh Beekeeper

A publication of the Welsh Beekeepers Association, giving news and views of beekeeping and related subjects. Articles and advertisements enquiries should be sent to the Editor. Articles written in Welsh should be sent to the Sub Editor. Gwenynwyr Cymru is provided free to members of Affiliated Associations and Individual Members. Information regarding subscriptions is available from the Individual Membership / Subscription Secretary.

IS-OLYGYDD (ERTHYGLAU
CYMRAEG)/SUB EDITOR
Dewi Morris Jones
Llwynderw, Bronant
Aberystwyth SY23 4TG
(01974 251264)

ARHOLIADAU/EXAMINATIONS
Dinah Sweet
Graig Fawr Lodge
Caerphilly
CF83 1NF
president@wbka.com

GWASANAETH CLYWELED / AUDIO-VISUAL AIDS SERVICE

This service is available to all affiliated associations and individual members. Further information is available from the Audio-Visual Aids Secretary.

DARLITHWYR / DANGOSWYR, LECTURERS / DEMONSTRATORS

The names and addresses of lecturers and demonstrators, recommended by associations affiliated to the WBKA, are available from the General Secretary.

CYNLLUN CYSWLLT CHWYSTRELLU / SPRAY LIAISON SCHEME

Information is available from the General secretary

SIOEAU / SHOWS

Honey/beekeeping sections are included at the Royal Welsh Agricultural Show, Llanelwedd, (OS ref: SO040520) during July, and at county, town and village shows throughout Wales. Information relating to these events may be obtained from secretaries of associations in the locality of the shows.

The historic FFAIR FEL ABERCONWY is held annually in the main street of the town, (OS ref: SH278378), on 13th September. Further information is available from the secretary of Conwy Association.

RHEOLAU CYFREITHIOL / STATUTORY REGULATIONS

The administration of the statutory regulations governing all aspects of beekeeping in Wales, is the responsibility of the Wales National Assembly, Caerdydd, CF99 1NA Phone (02920) 825111 Fax: (02920) 823352 Matters concerning statutory regulations, their implications and execution, should be addressed to the Minister of Agriculture and Rural Affairs, Wales National Assembly, at the above address.

THE.NATIONAL HONEY.SHOW

www.honeyshow.co.uk
THE 2012 SHOW IS AT ST GEORGE'S COLLEGE, WEYBRIDGE 27TH - 29TH OCTOBER

AELODAETH UNIGOL-TANYSGRIFAU/ INDIVIDUAL MEMBERSHIP SUBSCRIPTIONS

Jane Frank
61 Fir Court Ave
Churchstoke
Montgomery, Powys
SY15 6BA
01588 620711
janefrank@bluebottle.com

YSWIRIANT/INSURANCE CONTACT TREASURER FOR INFORMATION

INSURANCE:
Rhodri Powell
146 Pandy Rd, Bedwas,
Caerphilly CF83 8EP
rhodro@hotmail.com

AUDIO VISUAL AIDS:
F. G. Eckton
Cartref
Llanafan Fawr,
Llanfair ym Muallt LD2 3LT
01591 620456

CONVENTION SECRETARY:
John Page
john-of-pontsian@ tiscali.co.uk

CONVENTION TRADE STANDS SECRETARY:
Wally Shaw
Llwyn Ysgaw, Dwyran,
Llanfairpwll, Anglesey
LL61 6RH 01248 430811
waltershaw301@ btinternet.com

WBKA/CGC

✉ ☎

CYMDEITHASAU TADOGOL A'U YSGRIFENYDDION / AFFILIATED ASSOCIATIONS AND SECRETARIES

ABERYSTWYTH, Ann Ovens,
Tan-y-Cae, Nr Talybont,
Ceredigion,
SY24 5OL
01970 832359
ann.ovens@btinternet.com

ANGLESEY, Peter Edwards
Erw Newydd Llanfair ME
Tynygongl Ynys Mon
LL74 8NR
01248 853879
pwedw3@hotmail.co.uk

**BRECKNOCK AND RADNOR,
Dr Gillian Todd,** Meadow
Breeze, Llanddew, Brecon
LD3 9ST
01874610902 07971314798
gbtodd@btinternet.com

BRIDGEND, Sue Verran Ty Mel,
Maesteg Rd. Bridgend
CF32 0EE
01656 729699
verran@btinternet.com

**CARDIFF AND VALE, Annie
Newsam**
Stonecroft, Mountain Road,
Bedwas, Caerphilly, CF83 8ER
annienewsam@hotmail.co.uk

CARMARTHEN, Brian Jones
Cwmburry Honey Farm,
Ferryside, Carmarthenshire,
SA17 5TW
01267 267318
beegeejay2003@yahoo.co.uk

CONWY, Mr Peter McFadden,
Ynys Goch
Ty'n y Groes,
Conwy LL32 8UH
01492 650851
peter@honeyfair.freeserve.
co.uk

**EAST CARMARTHEN
John Williams,** Penrhiw,
Llansadwrn, Llanwrda,
SA19 8LP,
01550 777498,
john@penrhiw.net

**FLINT AND DISTRICT,
Jill and Graham Wheeler,**
Mertyn Downing, Whitford
Holywell, Flintshire,
CH8 9EP.
01745 560557
mertyndowning@btinternet.
com

**GWENYNWYR CYMRAEG
CEREDIGION W.I.Griffiths,**
Llain Deg, Comins Coch,
Aberystwyth, SY23 3BG
01970 623334
 wilmair@btinternet.com

**LAMPETER AND DISTRICT
Mr Gordon Lumby,**
Gwynfryn, Brynteg,
Llanybydder,
SA40 9UX
01570 480571
g.lumby@btopenworld.com

**LLEYN AC EIFIONYDD
Amanda Bristow,** Bryngwydion,
Pontllyfni, Gwynedd
LL54 5EY 01286 831328
amanda@vosltd.com

MEIRIONNYDD, Lesley Bay,
Hen Orsaf, Gellilydan,
Blaenau-ffestiniog,
LL41 4EP
01766 590488
bazurka@aol.com

MONTGOMERY, Jessica Bennett,
Plasheulwen, Llanfair Road,
Newtown, Powys,
SY16 3JY
01686 626872
jessica.bennett@virgin.net

PEMBROKESHIRE, Mr J Dudman,
Sevenoaks, The Kilns,
Llangwm, Haverfordwest,
Pembrokeshire,
SA62 4HG
01437 891892
secretarypbka@hotmail.com>

**SOUTH CLWYD,
Mrs Carol Keys-Shaw,** Y Beudy,
Maesmor Hall, Maerdy
Corwen LL21 0NS
01490 460592
c.keysshaw@btinternet.com

SWANSEA, Paul Lyons,
2 West Cliff, Southgate,
Swansea, SA3 2AN.
paul.lyons@bt.com

TEIFISIDE, John Page,
The Old Tannery, Pontsian,
Llandysul, SA44 4UD
01545 590515
john-of-pontsian@tiscali.
co.uk

WEST GLAMORGAN,
Mr John Beynon,
48, Whitestone Avenue,
Bishopston,
Swansea. SA3 3DA
01792 232810,
jakbeynon@btinternet.com

HEB DADOGU/NON
AFFILIATED:
Mrs J Bromley
Ty Hir, Monmouth Road
Raglan, Usk. NP15 2ET
01291 690331
bromleyjan@hotmail.com

BEIRNIAID SIOE FÊL TRWYDDEDIG / WBKA QUALIFIED HONEY SHOW

TERRY E. ASHLEY
Meadow Cottage,
11 Elton Lane, Winterley
Sandbach CW11 4TN
M. J. BADGER MBE
14 Thorn Lane, Leeds
LS8 1NN
M BESSANT
Gwili Lodge, Heol
Lotwen, Rhydaman
SA18 3RP
ROBERT BREWER
PO Box 369, Hiawassee,
Georgia, USA
TOM CANNING
151 Portadown Road,
Armagh, Co Armagh
BT61 9HL
LES CHIRNSIDE
Bryn-y-Pant Cottage,
Upper Llanover,
Abergavenny NP7 9ES

CARYS EDWARDS
Ty Cerrig, Ganllwyd,
Dolgellau LL40 2TN
IFOR C. EDWARDS
Lleifior, Pontrhydygroes,
Ystrad Meurig SY25 6DN
D.H. FERGUSON-THOMAS
Erwlon, Llanwrda
SA19 8HD
STEVEN GUEST
Bridge House, Hind
Heath Road, Sandbach,
CW11 3LY
HUGH MCBRIDE
11 Ballyloughan Park
Antrim BT43 5HW
LORRAINE MCBRIDE
11 Ballyloughan Park
Antrim BT43 5HW

CECIL MCMULLAN
33 Glebe Road,
Hillsborough, County
Down
LEO MCGUINESS
89 Dunlade Road, Grey
Steel BT47 4QL
GAIL ORR
64 Ballycrone Road,
Hillsborough BT26 6NH
Dinah Sweet
Graig Fawr Lodge,
Caerphilly, CF83 1NF
REDMOND WILLIAMS
Tincurry, Cahir, Co
Tipperary Eire
MICHAEL YOUNG MBE
Mileaway, Carnreagh,
Hillsborough BT26 6LJ

NBU

⊠ ☎

NATIONAL BEE UNIT, THE FOOD AND ENVIRONMENT RESEARCH AGENCY

www.nationalbeeunit.com

National Bee Unit
The Food and Environment
Research Agency
Sand Hutton, York, YO41
1LZ, UK

Tel.No: 01904 462510
Fax.No: 01904 462240
E-Mail: nbu@fera.gsi.gov.uk
Website:
www.nationalbeeunit.com
www.fera.defra.gov.uk
Policy :   www.defra.gov.uk

NATIONAL BEE UNIT TECHNICAL
STAFF, HEAD OF UNIT
Mike Brown

HOME BASED STAFF:

NATIONAL BEE INSPECTOR
Andy Wattam
01522 789726
07775 027524

NATIONAL BEE UNIT IS NOW UNDER THE FOOD AND ENVIRONMENT RESEARCH AGENCY (FERA)

NATIONAL BEE UNIT

The National Bee Unit (NBU) is part of the executive agency of the Department for Environment, Food and Rural Affairs (Defra), and is based just outside York. The Unit is an element of Fera's Inspectorate Programme and its work covers all aspects of bee health and husbandry in England and Wales, on behalf of Defra in England and for the Welsh Government in Wales. The work of the unit includes disease and pest diagnosis, research into bee health matters, development of contingency plans for emerging threats, import risk analysis, related extension work and consultancy services to both government and industry.

BEE HEALTH INSPECTION SERVICE

The Integrated Bee Health Programme is run by the NBU on behalf of core policy customers. The NBU has a long track record in bee husbandry and bee disease control (since 1946) and has been directly responsible for the bee inspection services in England and Wales since 1994.

The NBU consists of a home-based inspectorate team, and the laboratory diagnostic and research team based at Fera, York. In addition colleagues across Fera contribute to the programme and research projects.

The Bee Health Inspectorate

The inspectorate team consists of approximately 50 home-based members of staff. It is headed by the National Bee Inspector (NBI), whose role it is to manage the statutory disease control and training programmes. The NBI has management responsibility for eight home-

172

based Regional Bee Inspectors (RBIs), one heading each of the seven regions in England and one covering Wales. The RBI in turn manages a number of Seasonal Bee Inspectors (SBIs). The RBIs and SBIs organise inspections under EU and UK legislation, submit suspect samples for diagnosis, treat colonies for foul brood and train beekeepers in bee husbandry for better disease control and greater self-sufficiency. In addition the bee inspectors also collect honey samples for residue analysis under the Statutory Honey collection agreement with Defra Veterinary Medicines Directorate (VMD). With *Aethina tumida* (Small hive beetle (SHB)) and *Tropilaelaps* spp. both notifiable under UK and EU law inspectors also undertake surveillance for these exotics in "at risk apiaries" close to identified high risk areas.

BEE DISEASE DIAGNOSTIC TEAM

The NBU's diagnostic team provides a rapid, modern service for both the inspection team and beekeepers. The NBU laboratory is Good Laboratory Practice (GLP) compliant, a quality accreditation scheme administered by the Department of Health. All diagnostic tests are conducted according to the OIE (Office International des Epizooties) Manual of Standard Diagnostic Tests and Vaccines. The OIE is the world organisation for animal health and produce internationally recognised disease diagnosis guidelines (http//www.oie.int.) Across Fera diagnostic support is provided from teams of microbiologists acarologists, insect virologists and molecular specialists in the Fera Molecular Technology Unit (MTU).

BEES AND THE LAW

The Bees Act 1980 UK empowers Agriculture Ministers to make Orders to control pests and diseases affecting bees, and provides powers of entry for authorised persons. Under the Bees Act, The Bee Diseases and Pests Control Order 2006 for England and Wales, (there is similar legislation for Scotland and Northern Ireland) designates American foulbrood (AFB), European foulbrood (EFB), A. tumida (SHB) and Tropilaelaps mites

REGIONAL BEE INSPECTORS
Ian Molyneux
Northern Region
01204 381186
07775 119442

Dave Bonner (Acting RBI)
Western Region
07775 119434

Nigel Semmence
Southern Region
01264 338694
07776 493649

Alan Byham
South East Region
01306 611016
07775 119447

Adam Vevers
South West Region
01364 653474
07775 119453

Keith Morgan
Eastern Region
01485 520838
07919 004215

Ivor Flatman
North East Region
01924 252795
07775 119436

Frank Gellatly
Wales
01558 650663
07775 119480

FOR DETAILS OF SEASONAL
BEE INSPECTORS DETAILS
CONTACT THE RELEVANT RBI OR
CHECK BEEBASE

NBU

✉ ☎

LABORATORY BASED STAFF
Research Co-ordinator
Giles Budge

Commercial &
Diagnostics Manager
Selwyn Wilkins

Laboratory Manager
Ben Jones

Apiary Manager
Damian Cierniak

Administrative
Programme Support
Kate Parker,
Lesley Debenham &
Jenna Cook

(all species) as notifiable pests and defines the action which may be taken in the event of outbreaks.

At the European level, the Directive on animal health requirements for trade in bees is called the Balai Directive (92/65/EEC) implemented in the UK under the Animal and Animal Products (Import and Export) Regulations. It lists American foul brood (AFB), the small hive beetle (A. tumida) and Tropilaelaps mites as notifiable pests and diseases throughout the EU (at the time of writing time neither the small hive beetle nor Tropilaelaps have been confirmed in Europe).

THE IMPORTATION OF BEES

It is legal to import Queen bees from third countries, the rules governing this are set out in Commission Decision 2003/881/EC, as amended by Commission Decision 2005/60/EC. The list of countries is currently restricted to, Argentina, Australia and New Zealand.

It is legal to import bees freely from the EU (including queens, packages and colonies). Under the Balai directive consignments of bees moved between Member States must be accompanied by an original health certificate confirming freedom from notifiable pests and diseases.

For full details on the importation of bees from within the EU or from Third countries please either consult the Defra website, BeeBase or contact the NBU.

AMERICAN AND EUROPEAN FOUL BROOD

Foul brood-infected apiaries are placed under standstill notice, supervised by the bee inspector, until the disease is cleared from the apiary and the honey from antibiotic-treated colonies is safe to harvest. We always aim to minimise the impact of this as far as possible, in co-operation with the beekeeper.

VARROA

As part of the NBU's routine field screening programme the first known case of pyrethroid resistant varroa mites in the UK was discovered in apiaries in Devon in August 2001. The NBU undertook a resistance-monitoring programme throughout England and Wales. Pyrethroid resistant Varroa mites are now widespread in England and Wales. To access current advice on Varroa and Varroa Management please visit BeeBase.

ADULT BEE DISEASES

The NBU also look for adult bee diseases and parasites such as Nosema species (*Nosema apis* and *Nosema. ceranae*, amoeba (*Malpighamoeba mellificae*) and tracheal mites (*Acarine* or *Acarapis woodi*) from samples submitted by beekeepers. As these diseases are non-statutory this service is chargeable. For the current cost please contact the NBU or visit the website.. Bees that have been imported from designated Third countries are also checked for disease and are also screened for exotic pests potentially harmful to UK beekeeping.

EXOTICS

Beekeepers must make themselves aware of the potential threats to beekeeping in the UK. The field inspection team monitors for potential exotics, the SHB and Tropilaelaps spp. The laboratory team also routinely screen import samples and suspect samples submitted for identification by both beekeepers and the field team.

PESTICIDE MONITORING

The Wildlife Incident Investigation Scheme (WIIS) is a unique scheme for monitoring the effects of pesticides on wildlife, including beneficial invertebrates such as honey bees. It is led by the Chemicals Regulation Directorate (CRD) with Natural England managing and undertaking site enquiries on their behalf; The Food and Environment Research Agency (Fera) carry out disease and pesticide analysis and, if appropriate, the Veterinary Laboratories Agency (VLA) carry out post mortems on wildlife. Information gathered is fed into the approval process for pesticides and helps in the verification and improvement of pesticide risk assessments.

It can also result in changes to label recommendations on pesticide products. It is not provided as a personal service to beekeepers wishing to seek evidence for the purpose of civil litigation but can lead to enforcement action being taken by the enforcer if the misuse or abuse of a product is identified as part of this process. For more information please see the website.

RESEARCH & DEVELOPMENT

A programme of research and development within the group underpins the Unit's work. They also have long-established links with many European and world wide research centres, universities and the beekeeping industry. The primary aim of our R&D is to improve our understanding of the issues which impact bee health. The NBU also actively supports PhD students, some of which are funded using donations from the beekeeping industry. For an update on the current R&D work of the unit please see BeeBase.

RISK ASSESSMENT

The National Bee Unit manages 150 honey bee colonies and has much experience in assessing the effects and efficacy of veterinary bee medicines (e.g., varroacides) and pesticides in both field and laboratory tests. Our Good Laboratory Practice (GLP) accreditation allows us to undertake a wide range of routine and specially designed laboratory, semi-field and field studies on honeybees and bumblebees for regulatory authorities and industry worldwide.

EXTENSION

The NBU trains beekeepers in several ways: local courses and advisory visits run by the inspectors, and national courses held at the York laboratory. The NBU annually hosts the National Diploma in Beekeeping residential courses and has also been host to visiting overseas workers and researchers. NBU York based staff also provide training to beekeepers at local and regional beekeeper meetings.

HEALTHY BEES PLAN

The Healthy Bees Plan was published by Defra and the Welsh Assembly Government in March 2009 following consultation with beekeepers and the main Beekeeping Associations. It sets out a plan for Government, beekeepers and other stakeholders to work together to respond effectively to pest and disease threats and to put in place programmes to ensure a sustainable and productive future for beekeeping In England and Wales.

The Healthy Bees Plan consists of three working groups that report to the project management board to help deliver the five major objectives of the plan. To view the Healthy Bees Plan, please see the website.

(This is the most recent information received from the National Bee Unit).

BeeBase is the National Bee Unit website. It is designed for beekeepers and supports Defra, WAG and Scotland's Bee Health Programmes and the Healthy Bees Plan, which set out to protect and sustain our valuable national bee stocks.

Our website provides a wide range of free information for beekeepers, to help keep their honey bees healthy.

We hope both new and experienced beekeepers will find this an extremely useful resource and sign up to BeeBase. Knowing the distribution of beekeepers and their apiaries across the country helps us to effectively monitor and control the spread of serious honey bee pests and diseases, as well as provide up-to-date information in keeping bees healthy and productive. By telling us who you are you'll be playing a very important part in helping to maintain and sustain honey bees for the future.

To register as a beekeeper please visit BeeBase.

DARD/NI

✉ ☎

DEPARTMENT OF AGRICULTURE AND RURAL DEVELOPMENT FOR NORTHERN IRELAND

WWW.dardni.gov.uk

BEE DISEASE DIAGNOSTICS:
Sam Clawson
Agri-Food and Biosciences
Institute (AFBI)
Newforge Lane
BELFAST BT9 5PX
Tel: 028 9025 5289
Email: Sam.Clawson@
afbini.gov.uk

TRAINING COURSES:
Jennifer Ball
Greenmount Campus
College of Agriculture Food
and Rural Enterprise:
Information is available
from the College at
Tel: 028 9442 6879
Text phone: 028 9052 4420
Email: jennifer.ball@
dardni.gov.uk

BEE INSPECTIONS:
Thomas Williamson
Quality Assurance Branch,
DARD, Manor House
Loughall, Co Armagh
Tel: 028 3889 2374
Fax: 028 3889 2382
Email: Thomas.williamson@
dardni.gov.uk

Honeybee Regional Report for Northern Ireland 2007

Bee Health Surveys

A questionnaire survey for Bee Husbandry issues was circulated to beekeepers via beekeeping associations. This was done in April 2009, 2010 and 2011. The results of the 2010 survey are available as a pdf on the AFBI website (www.afbini.gov.uk). This showed colony losses for 2010 were 13% compared to 23% in 2009. Forty-four percent of beekeepers reported no losses. The 2011 survey results are currently being processed but will be available on the AFBI website in November.

Bee Health Inspections

The Bee Inspectorate carried out surveys for American foul brood, European foul brood, Small Hive beetle and Tropilaelaps mite along with resistance testing of varroa mites to pyrethroids. American foul brood outbreaks reduced sharply with eight apiaries found to have the disease to date compared to twenty apiaries in 2010. Many of the outbreaks were in east of the province in apiaries which had no record of the disease before. No cases of European foul brood were recorded, although a number of hives were checked using field test kits and laboratory analysis. Surveys continued for Small Hive Beetle and Tropilaelaps mite. Apiaries in the vicinity of ports or fruit importers were targeted for Small Hive Beetle inspections using corriboard shelter traps, while apiaries that had imported in the past were selected and hive scrapings examined for Tropilaelaps mite.

Varroa

Varroa is virtually ubiquitous in Northern Ireland, consequently no systematic studies of prevalence are conducted. Samples continue to be submitted to monitor varroacide resistance. One sample returned a borderline result, which, although not conclusive, means that varroacide resistance is likely to be a future problem.

Adult Bee Disease Diagnostics

Nosema ceranae was first recorded in Northern Ireland in 2010. *Nosema ceranae* is an emergent pathogen of western honeybees. It is similar to the endemic species, *Nosema apis* but is considered to produce a more virulent disease than *N. apis,* probably reflecting its more recent association with the western honeybee. Samples submitted and positive for *Nosema* are screened for *N. ceranae* on an ad-hoc basis. To date, 62 samples were received and tested with 23 (37%) containing *N. ceranae*. Note, however, this should not be used as an indicator of prevalence, as samples were not spatially representative of colony distribution in Northern Ireland.

Up to September 2011, 70 samples have been submitted to the laboratory, with 22 positive for Nosema and 13 positive for acarine. In 2010, we had a total of 96 possible disease samples from QAB/beekeepers submitted to the laboratory.

Residue Sampling

Honey samples were again lifted this year for testing for residues of veterinary medicines and environmental contaminants. Samples lifted last year were found to be satisfactory.

Imports

Eighty direct Queen imports were notified to DARD in 2011. Indirect imports through England were also noted by the inspectorate during routine inspections. Imports have mainly originated in Slovenia, Greece and Denmark.

A number of follow-up inspections were carried out to check records and health certificates for notified imports along with investigations to establish legality of other suspected bee movements.

The Bee Diseases and Pests Control Order (Northern Ireland) 2007
The above Order came into operation on the 21 May 2007, which brought our list of notifiable pests and diseases into line with England and Wales.

Bee Health Contingency Plan
The Bee Health Contingency Plan is reviewed annually and an updated version was published on the DARD Internet in May 2011.

Strategy for the Sustainability of the Honey Bee
The Strategy for the Sustainability of the Honey Bee was published in February 2011 and aims to achieve a sustainable and healthy population of honey bees for both pollination and honey production in the north of Ireland through strengthened partnership working between Government and Stakeholders. The Strategy confirms DARD's ongoing commitment to help protect and improve the health of honey bees and support the sector in its efforts to sustain and support beekeeping. The Ulster Beekeepers Association (UBKA) and the Institute of NI Beekeepers (INIB) have made a commitment to support the Strategy intentions. The Strategy is aimed at both policy makers and beekeepers, and importantly, identifies the roles and responsibilities of the different stakeholders in delivering its aims and outcomes. It seeks to address the current challenges facing beekeepers and provides a plan of action aimed at sustaining the health of honey bees and beekeeping in the north of Ireland for the next decade.

The Strategy for the Sustainability of the Honey Bee can be viewed at:
http://www.dardni.gov.uk/index/publications/pubs-dard-fisheries-farming-and-food/publications-dard-strategy-for-the-sustainability-of-the-honey-bee.htm

Jim Crummie
Senior Bee Health Officer, DARD
Thomas Williamson
Senior Bee Inspector, DARD
Sam Clawson
Bee Disease Diagnostics, AFBI
Seamus Hughes
Farm Policy Branch, DARD

SGRPID

✉ ☎

THE SCOTTISH GOVERNMENT RURAL PAYMENTS AND INSPECTIONS DIRECTORATE BEE INSPECTORS

HEADQUARTERS
Lead Bee Inspector
Stephen Sunderland,
P Spur, Saughton House,
Broomhouse Drive,
Edinburgh, EH11 3XD
Tel: 0300 244 6672
e-mail: beesmailbox@
scotland.gsi.gov.uk

The Scottish Government (SG) is responsible for bee health policy in Scotland. SG recognises the importance of a strong bee health programme, not only for the production of honey, but also for the contribution that bees make to the pollination of many crop species and to the wider environment.

Honeybees are susceptible to a variety of threats, including pests and diseases, the likelihood and consequences of which have increased significantly over the last few years. The Scottish Government takes very seriously any biosecurity threat to the sustainability of the apiculture sector and is working closely with colleagues in Food and Environment Research Agency's (Fera) National Bee Unit (NBU) to enable a more joined up approach to be taken throughout Great Britain on the issues surrounding bee health.

The Scottish Government has invested in the NBU's national web based database for beekeepers "BeeBase" and actively encourages beekeepers to register onto the system. This service will provide bee health and disease outbreak information and will also assist Bee Inspectors in disease control. BeeBase also provides information on legislation, pests and disease recognition and control, interactive maps, current research areas and key contacts.

Beekeepers have a significant role to play in ensuring disease management and control within their own apiaries are in order as they have a legal obligation to report any suspicion of a notifiable disease or pest to the Bee Inspector at their local Scottish Government Rural Payments Inspections Directorate (SGRPID) Area Office.

The Bee Inspectors, based at Area Offices of SGRPID, are responsible for the operation of The Bee Diseases and Pests

Control (Scotland) Order 2007 in their area with duties including:-
- inspection of apiaries for presence of statutory bee diseases
- taking and delivering samples to SASA,
- issuing and removal of 'Standstill Notices'
- issuing of 'Destruction Notices' and supervising destruction
- informing beekeepers of treatment options for European Foul Brood (EFB), where appropriate
- granting the option, after taking account of the recommendations of SASA, and carrying out treatment
- carrying out follow-up inspections after destruction or treatment

SASA

Science and Advice for Scottish Agriculture (SASA) is responsible for providing specialist technical support and is authorised under The Bee Diseases and Pests Control (Scotland) Order 2007 as "SASA". Duties include:

- examination of submitted samples suspected of being infected with American Foul Brood, European Foul Brood, Small Hive Beetle (SHB) or *Tropilaelaps*.
- reporting results on which pathogen or pest is present
- recommending, in consultation with the Bee Inspector, the most suitable option, destruction or treatment, for each individual case of EFB.
- where treatment is agreed, ordering supplies of the approved antibiotic
- provision of a free diagnostic service to beekeepers to identify and confirm presence of varroa.
- maintaining technical liaison with National Bee Unit, The Food and Environment Research Agency, Sand Hutton, York, providing technical documentation as required
- providing training courses and demonstration material as required

SASA (SCIENCE AND ADVICE FOR SCOTTISH AGRICULTURE)
1 Roddinglaw Rd,
Edinburgh, EH12 9FJ
BEE DISEASES,
FIONA HIGHET
Plant Health Section
(0131) 244 8817
PESTICIDE INCIDENTS,
ELIZABETH SHARP
Chemistry Section
(0131) 244 8874

PESTICIDE INCIDENTS

As part of the Wildlife Incident Investigation Scheme, SASA undertakes analytical investigations into bee mortalities where pesticide poisoning may have been involved. Beekeepers should send samples of dead bees (200) direct to SASA, Chemistry Section, for analysis. In the case of major incidents, beekeepers are advised to contact their nearest SGRPID Area Office so that an early field investigation can be instigated.

SGRPID

✉ ☎

THE FOLLOWING SCOTTISH GOVERNMENT RURAL PAYMENTS AND INSPECTIONS DIRECTORATE (SGRPID) STAFF ARE AUTHORISED BEE INSPECTORS. ALL BEE INSPECTORS HAVE EMAIL ADDRESSES AS "FIRSTNAME.SURNAME@SCOTLAND.GSI.GOV.UK"

SOUTHERN -
DUMFRIES AREA OFFICE,
Angus Cameron
161 Brooms Road, Dumfries
DG1 3ES
(01387) 274400
Fax: (01387) 274440

SOUTH EASTERN -
GALASHIELS AREA OFFICE,
Angus MacAskill
Cotgreen Road,
Tweedbank, Galashiels,
Scottish Borders, TD1 3SG
(01896) 892400
Fax: (01896) 892424

SOUTH WESTERN -
AYR AREA OFFICE,
John Smith
Russell House, King Street,
Ayr, South Ayrshire,
KA8 0BG
(01292) 291300
Fax: (01292) 291301

EDINBURGH (HQ)
Steve Sunderland
P Spur, Saughton House,
Broomhouse Drive,
Edinburgh.
EH11 3XD
0300 244 6672
Fax: 0300 244 9797

GRAMPIAN - INVERURIE
AREA OFFICE,
Kirsteen Sutherland
Thainstone Court,
Inverurie, Grampian,
Aberdeenshire, AB51 5YA
(01467) 626247
Fax: (01467) 626217

GRAEME SHARPE, APICULTURE
Specialist, Veterinary
Services, SAC,
Auchincruive, Ayr.
Tel:01292 525375

SCOTTISH AGRICULTURAL COLLEGE (SAC)

The Scottish Government supports a full-time apiculture specialist (Graeme Sharpe) who provides free of charge comprehensive advisory, training and education programmes for beekeepers throughout Scotland on all aspects of Integrated Pest Management and good husbandry including the control of Varroa. Graeme also promotes awareness of notifiable bee diseases and pests and the provision of general advice of good husbandry and management practices to ensure healthy honeybee colonies.

WWW.SCOTLAND.GOV.UK/TOPICS/APICULTURE/GRANTS/INSPECTIONS/BEEINSPECTIONS

USEFUL TABLES

BEEKEEPING METRIC CONVERTION TABLES

°CENT	FAHR	INCH	MM	INCH	MM	INCH	MM
0	32	$1/25$	1	$1^5/8$	42	10	254
5	40	$1/12$	2	$1^{11}/16$	43	$10^1/4$	260
7	44	$1/8$	3	$1^9/20$	48	$11^1/4$	286
30	86	$1/16$	5	2	51	$11^1/2$	292
34	92	$1/4$	6	3	76	$11^3/4$	298
38	100	$5/16$	8	$4^1/4$	108	12	305
43	110	$3/8$	9	$4^1/2$	114	14	356
49	120	$1/2$	12.5	$4^3/4$	121	$16^1/4$	413
54	130	$5/8$	16	$5^1/2$	140	$16^1/2$	49
60	140	$3/4$	18	$5^3/4$	146	17	431
62	144	$7/8$	22	6	152	$17^5/8$	448
82	180	1	25	$6^1/4$	159	$18^1/8$	460
90	194	$1^1/16$	27	$8^1/4$	216	$18^1/4$	483
100	212	$1^3/8$	35	$8^3/4$	223	20	508
		$1^9/20$	37	$9^1/8$	232	$21^1/2$	546
		$1^1/2$	38	$9^3/8$	239	$21^3/4$	552
				$9^9/16$	246	22	559

INTERNATIONAL QUEEN MARKING COLOURS

YEAR ENDING	COLOUR	REMEMBER
1 & 6	WHITE	Will
2 & 7	YELLOW	You
3 & 8	RED	Raise
4 & 9	GREEN	Good
5 & 0	BLUE	Bees?

BOTTOM BEE-SPACE HIVES

No, of cells in brood box
Lug length (MM)
Frame spacing (mm)
Frame size (mm)
No. frames
Hive tvpe

Hive type		No. frames	Frame size (mm)	Frame spacing (mm)	Lug length (MM)	No. of cells in brood box
National	BROOD	11	356 x 216	37	38	58000
	SUPER	10	356 x 140	42	38	36000
Modified Commercial	BROOD	11	406 x 254	37	16	75000
	SUPER	10	406 x 152	42	16	

TOP BEE-SPACE HIVES

No, of cells in brood box
Lug length (MM)
Frame spacing (mm)
Frame size (mm)
No. frames
Hive tvpe

Hive type		No. frames	Frame size (mm)	Frame spacing (mm)	Lug length (MM)	No. of cells in brood box
Smith	BROOD	11	356 x 216	37	18	58000
	SUPER	10	356 x 140	42	18	36000
Langstroth	BROOD	10	448 x 232	35	16	68000
	SUPER	10	448 x 140	35	16	
Jumbo	BROOD	10	448 x 286	35	16	85000
	SUPER	10	448 x 140	35	16	
Modified Dadant	BROOD	11	448 x 286	37	16	93000
	SUPER	10	448 x 159	42	16	

USEFUL TABLES

CONVERSION FACTORS

TEMPERATURE

Fahrenheit > Celcius (Centigrade)	- 32, x 0.5555 ($^5/_9$)
Celcius > Fahrenheit	x 1.8 ($^9/_5$), + 32

WEIGHT

Ounces > Pounds	x 28.3495
Pounds > Grams	x 453.59237
Hundredweights > Kilograms	x 50.8
Grams > Ounces	⁒ 28.3495
Kilograms > Pounds	x 2.2142

LENGTH

Inches > Centimetres	x 2.54
Yards > Metres	x 0.9144
Miles > Kilometres	x 1.609
Centimetres > Inches	x 0.3937
Metres > Yards	x 1.0936
Kilometres > Miles	⁒ 1.609

AREA

Acres > Hectares	x 0.404686
Hectares > Acres	x 2.47105

VOLUMN

Pints > Litres	x 0.5683
Gallons > Litres	x 4.546
Litres > Pints	x 1.7598
Litres > Gallons	x 0.21997

Notes

www.ingramcontent.com/pod-product-compliance
Lightning Source LLC
Chambersburg PA
CBHW071222290326
41931CB00037B/1849